MW00584456

"If the church in North America does not discover the New Testament ethos of multiethnic community, the church in North America will fail in accomplishing its mission. I know of no better voice to show us the way than my friend Bryan Loritts. In his new book *The Offensive Church*, Bryan shows us the way forward rooted in a gospel-centered missiology of making disciples in community. This is a must-read for anyone serious about joining in God's activity in North America and the nations!"

Vance Pitman, president of Send Network and founding pastor of Hope Church Las Vegas

"One of the many radical things Jesus taught was that his followers must learn to love across the lines of difference, or what some call enemy lines. In Christ there is now no longer any Jew or Gentile, male or female, slave or free, for we are all one in Christ Jesus. In tearing down these and other dividing walls of hostility through his death on the cross, Jesus provided not only an example of what it means to love one's enemies but also the resources that empower us to do so ourselves. In a world filled with racial tension and discord, my friend Bryan Loritts does a tremendous job helping us unlock those resources and showing us how to love in the power of Christ."

Scott Sauls, senior pastor of Christ Presbyterian Church and author of *Jesus Outside the Lines*

"Bryan Loritts's vision for discipleship is an urgent word for the American church. His plea to 'play a redemptive offense modeled after the words and example of Jesus' should be heard widely because Christians today need boldness and deep faith to become all we're called to be together. This book skillfully readies us to pursue the challenge of real reconciliation that God desires for his people."

Tony Evans, senior pastor of Oak Cliff Bible Fellowship and president of the Urban Alternative

"The racial and political upheaval of our day is causing Christians to abandon the pursuit of beautiful community, the ministry of reconciliation in Jesus' name. In *The Offensive Church*, Bryan Loritts raises his voice, 'Not so fast!' With winsome grace he calls us out of contentment in ecclesial ghettos to embrace the reconciling power of our Savior, proclaiming and practicing a robust gospel in our divided world."

Irwyn L. Ince Jr., author of *The Beautiful Community: Unity, Diversity, and the Church at Its Best*

"Since becoming the codirector of the Winsome Conviction Project, I've attempted to facilitate civil conversations between Christians. Simply put, race is in its own category. At the mere mention of race, people immediately voice anger, confusion, hurt, and defensiveness. Like no other topic, it shuts down communication and erects walls. What is most needed today is a trusted guide who doesn't shy away from the complexity of race but offers hope and a plan to open lines of communication. I can think of no one better qualified than Bryan Loritts to be our guide."

Tim Muehlhoff, professor of communication at Biola University and author of *Winsome Conviction: Disagreeing Without Dividing the Church*

THE OFFENSIVE CHURCH

BREAKING THE CYCLE OF ETHNIC DISUNITY

BRYAN C. LORITTS

An imprint of InterVarsity Press
Downers Grove, Illinois

InterVarsity Press
P.O. Box 1400 | Downers Grove, IL 60515-1426
ivpress.com | email@ivpress.com

InterVarsity Press® is the publishing division of InterVarsity Christian Fellowship/USA®. For more information, visit intervarsity.org.

Scripture quotations, unless otherwise noted, are from The Holy Bible, English Standard Version, copyright © 2001 by Crossway Bibles, a division of Good News Publishers. Used by permission. All rights reserved.

While any stories in this book are true, some names and identifying information may have been changed to protect the privacy of individuals.

Published in association with the literary agency of Wolgemuth & Associates.

The publisher cannot verify the accuracy or functionality of website URLs used in this book beyond the date of publication.

Cover design: David Fassett
Interior design: Daniel van Loon

ISBN 978-1-5140-0597-2 (print) | ISBN 978-1-5140-0599-6 (digital)

Printed in the United States of America ∞

Library of Congress Cataloging-in-Publication Data
A catalog record for this book is available from the Library of Congress.

30 29 28 27 26 25 24 23 | 12 11 10 9 8 7 6 5 4 3 2 1

TO MELO AND NICOLE SAUVAL

and the wonderful people of
One Family Church in Apopka, Florida

CONTENTS

INTRODUCTION

WHAT'S GOING ON?

IN 1971, MARVIN GAYE RELEASED *What's Going On?*, an album ranked by *Rolling Stone* as the greatest of all time. Surveying the sociological landscape, Gaye asked why so many Blacks were dying in the streets, spoke against the war in Vietnam, appealed to the power of love, and tackled issues of police brutality and racism.

Now let's say Gaye's album never saw the light of day. If I proposed an idea for a record based on issues today—policing, racism, poverty, and injustice—record executives would think, *This will resonate deeply*, not knowing I would only need to cut and paste Gaye's classic.

What Gaye sang about decades ago remains relevant today. His question is not only apropos of the broader culture but also the church of Jesus Christ and the new humanity Paul discusses in Ephesians 2.

What's going on with the body of Christ as we've become more and more divided over the issue of race?

What's going on when some of our White evangelical siblings who never talk about injustice suddenly start talking about critical race theory?

What's going on when a biblical term like *justice* is boot-legged by our culture and politics and returned to us as an expletive denoting a liberal?

What's going on when people are able to separate a political person, like Trump, from his political party but are unable to disentangle "Black lives matter" the sentiment from Black Lives Matter the organization?

What's going on with Christians who seem to filter their Bible through their politics and not their politics through their Bible?

What's going on with minorities who leave White or multi-ethnic spaces and look down on other minorities who choose to stay?

What's going on when leaders who lived through Jim Crow claim that "wokeness" is the greatest threat to the church in their lifetime?

And what's going on when I get thanked for preaching against abortion on Sanctity of Life Sunday but get called a social justice warrior on Martin Luther King Jr. weekend when I preach against racism?

If I sound like an alarmist, please know things are actually worse. A study led by James Davison Hunter published in November 2020 revealed that, since 1998, multiethnic churches in conservative evangelical spaces have tripled in number in the United States. This study also revealed

the widest divisions in America are, in fact, between White Evangelicals and the African American community as a whole. It is a racial chasm, to be sure, but one intensified and deepened by the particular character of conservative White Evangelicalism—a chasm not mirrored between Black Evangelicals and non-Evangelicals. This division is seen most sharply on those issues that specifically bear on African Americans and Hispanics as well.[1]

Think about that for a moment. The two most divided groups in the United States are not Democrats and Republicans, Protestants and Catholics, or even the Chicago Bears and Green Bay Packers (although my Chicago Bears–loving wife indicates otherwise by her actions), but *Blacks and conservative White evangelicals.*

When this study was released, I was driving around the suburbs of my father's home in Atlanta. My father was particularly reflective that day, as my siblings and I were in town to celebrate his retirement. His ministry began in the mid-1960s when he surrendered his life to Christ. Shortly thereafter, he enrolled in a Bible college to follow his call to preach. On the evening of April 4, 1968, word spread around his campus that Dr. Martin Luther King Jr. had been assassinated. My father's Bible college said and did nothing. No moment of silence. No change in chapel program. No singing of Dr. King's favorite gospel song, "Precious Lord."

A few years after graduation, my father joined the staff of what was then Campus Crusade for Christ, now known as Cru. For years he pushed for more minorities to join the fold, and some did. Later, he became the first Black pastor of an upper middle class White church in the northern suburbs of Atlanta. Fifteen years of his shepherding had transformed the church into a multiethnic community determined to keep the momentum going.

Yet, that day as we drove around my father's neighborhood—which is down the street from where many Asians had been killed just weeks earlier—we were reminded that the problem of race in America transcends the Black/White binary. Looking through the rearview of his life and ministry just days before his final sermon, my father wearily declared that race relations in the body of Christ were worse now than they had ever been in his lifetime.

The church of Jesus Christ has been playing offense, but in all the wrong ways. Instead of playing offense by actively loving one another, we have believed the worst about each other. Where we should be playing offense by aggressively seeking reconciliation, we have instead erected walls of division. We need to play a redemptive offense modeled after the words and example of Jesus.

Jesus' final prayer before the cross was a plea for oneness among his followers. Today, I might have more fortune praying to win the lottery than for oneness among Jesus' followers. But who or what is the culprit for this seismic rift in the body of Christ? The fault line is present and the earthquake is happening . . . right now.

I fear if followers of Jesus do not act, the strides taken over the last twenty years in the multiethnic church will be irreversibly revoked. It's one thing to have never tasted, quite another to have tasted and walked away.

I believe the solution is a matter of discipleship, but not as we know it. To be a disciple is to be a learner and to live like Jesus, imitating his example. The problem is that individualistic discipleship in the Western world is not the kind of discipleship Jesus envisioned. When we think of discipling someone, we envision showing them how to read their Bible, pray, steward their money, and understand what life in the Spirit looks like. We teach them about grace, the substitutionary work of Jesus Christ, and what justification and sanctification mean.

Yes and amen to these things! But they are not all discipleship is. Christian discipleship has its origins in Eastern culture, which values the communal far more than Western culture does. Dallas Willard's diagnosis was right: the problem with Christianity is we've made converts but not disciples. Jesus' paradigm for disciple making was not a succession of one-on-one meetings; instead, he formed a group of twelve very different individuals, teaching them to follow him and to love one another.

Although they were ethnically homogeneous (all Jewish men), they possessed profound differences. Their group comprised fishermen, tax collectors, and even a Zealot. When they jockeyed for position and power with one another, Jesus patiently waded into their humanity and called them not to the low ethic of tolerance, but to the high ethic of love.

Jesus also challenged their Jewish assumptions. He took them to Samaria, where he broke with ethnic, gender, and cultural norms by talking to a woman at the well. They watched in shock as Jesus challenged the Pharisees, the religious giants of their day. The disciples were pensive as Jesus greenlighted them to pick grain on the Sabbath. Together, these men were being formed into a Christocentric community filled with love, grace, and truth. The result would be a synergistic oneness unleashed on the world in the book of Acts. Though they often faced the powerful forces of culture and race that threatened to divide them—such as the Hellenistic and Hebraic controversy in Acts 6 and the question of Gentiles having to act like Jews in Acts 15— these men who had followed Jesus for three years stood as one, refusing the enemy's attempt to gain a foothold and divide the church.

But there's more. The first-century norm was a multiethnic church. Paul preached Jesus in Jewish synagogues *and* popular Gentile gathering places. Both groups responded to the gospel, and instead of starting two churches, Paul formed one local assembly and called them to work out horizontally what God in Christ had already accomplished for them vertically: reconciliation. Paul wrote them letters of encouragement and direction in the years to come. These letters serve as a model for a robust disciple-making strategy. In almost every instance, Paul begins by showing them what their relationship with God must look like. Then he pivots by claiming these things must be worked out in their relationships with others (Romans 12–16; Ephesians 4–6; Colossians 3–4). "Others" referred to ethnic others, as most of the churches Paul wrote to were multiethnic. So, to be discipled communally is to be discipled into a new humanity witnessed by the coming together of former enemies—Jews and Gentiles.

The problem of race in America can never be truly remedied without a commitment to disciple people both vertically and horizontally. As long as the homogeneous church is the norm, we will continue to chase our tails in a dizzying circle, ready to pass out over the problem of race. Even more maddening is that the growth of the multiethnic church, from 7 percent to 22 percent, has yielded little to no fruit with regard to the problem of race. Simply getting people of different ethnicities to sit, sing, and take notes in the same space is not enough. There is a profound difference between diversity and ethnic unity. What's missing is communal discipleship in which we are formed in the way of Jesus and into the new humanity with one another.

If there's one thing my years of working in and consulting with other churches desiring to be multiethnic has taught me, it's that we don't know each other across the ethnic divide. When clips of George Floyd's murder were playing over and over on the television, one of my sons, seething with anger, declared all White people were bad. While validating his anger, I also reminded him of the many dinners we had shared with our White friends and how good people like Uncle Adam and Aunt Nikki had been to us. These and many other White friends I've traversed the terrain of life with have kept me from such sweeping indictments. Transformative healing and power come from simply doing life together. Truly, we hurt in isolation but heal in community.

When it comes to matters of race, I have seen that most churches are composed of three groups: the ready, the resistant, and the reluctant. The resistant ain't reading this and have no plans to. The fact that you have this book in your hands means you probably skew toward ready: you're in a three-point stance, eager to take these things to your pastor, leader, or congregation and get a plan together.

In working with Christian organizations and churches over the last several decades, I've concluded that the biggest group is the reluctant. They're open in varying degrees to the discussion but are highly cautious. While they're naturally immature in their thinking, they can be brought along with the right leadership, pace, and discipleship. The reluctant need a shepherd, not a prophet.

In the aftermath of George Floyd's death, I fielded several calls from distraught leaders who, filled with prophetic fire, had stood before their White congregations with the purest of motives, denouncing White privilege and declaring Black lives matter and the need for reparations. They even announced that if the people weren't on the same page, they should question the legitimacy of their faith. The problem with this approach is that the people in those congregations had never been discipled communally into these things. The leaders went from zero to seventy in a matter of seconds. Unable to deal with the pastoral whiplash, the reluctant looked for the exits en masse.

Jesus didn't just send Peter to Cornelius the Gentile's home to preach the gospel. No—he prepared him by first sending him to the home of Simon the Tanner and called him to work these things out in a communal context. At first hesitant, Peter ultimately embraced the call to take the gospel cross-ethnically to the Gentiles, crossing over from a reluctant to a ready posture. The result was a multiethnic revival.

I write *The Offensive Church* to outfit you with what you need to move from reluctant to ready. A return to communal discipleship demands courageous, reliable leadership and relational environments. It's time the church of Jesus Christ stop reacting to the problem of race and instead lead proactively by discipling people into the new humanity.

CHAPTER ONE

PLAYING OFFENSE

IN 1883, A REAL ESTATE DEVELOPER named Horace Wilcox moved his family from the Midwest to Southern California, where he purchased a plot of land nestled closely to the Santa Monica hills, a few miles from Los Angeles. A devout follower of Jesus, Wilcox envisioned living out his utopian visions of the kingdom there. Hoping the church would transform the culture, he later gave away parcels of this land to denominations so they could build their churches.

Wilcox's wife chose to name the place after her favorite Midwestern estate: Hollywood. Yep, you read that right. On the very ground where Wilcox and his family sought to advance a kingdom that would shake up the world, another cultural juggernaut arose whose forces we continue to feel to this day. While I wholeheartedly affirm the dignity of all work and the need for Jesus-loving people to be a part of what is now more metaphorically known as Hollywood, Wilcox's vision is undeniably at odds with Hollywood's reality.

Score one for the culture.

One afternoon many centuries before Wilcox took a gander at his property, Jesus marched into Caesarea Philippi with

his followers. To put it mildly, Caesarea Philippi was not syn-
onymous with all things Christian, or even Jewish. At the
center of the town stood a rock platform for the famous Fes-
tival of Pan, where all kinds of immoral acts were on full display
for tens of thousands.

I've been to Caesarea Philippi, where not far from this rock
platform is a little hillside. Perhaps the disciples sat there
when Jesus asked them, "Who do you think the Son of Man
is?" Peter nailed it by declaring Jesus to be the Messiah.
Excitedly, Jesus responded, "And I tell you, you are Peter, and
on this rock I will build my church, and the gates of hell shall
not prevail against it" (Matthew 16:18). If you've been around
church, you understand the nature of the rock in this verse is
the subject of great debate. Catholics have historically said
the rock is Peter, as he went on to preach on the day of Pentecost and saw thousands come to faith and the church come
into being. On the other hand, Protestants have historically
claimed the rock is Peter's confession. After all, Paul said
Jesus is the cornerstone of the church (Ephesians 2:20).

These are good answers, but I think there's a better one.
Sitting on the hillside not far from the prominent rock
platform the afternoon I spent in Caesarea Philippi, I listened as our guide read from Matthew 16. When he got to
the part where Jesus says, "and on this rock," he pointed to
the rock platform—a simple but profound gesture that revo-
lutionized my thinking on the text and on the church. Jesus'
church would be built in immoral places. Jesus' church
would not inhabit sterile environments where it would
function as some foreign embassy detached from its sur-
rounding culture. Jesus' church is meant to occupy the world

and transform the culture rather than the culture trans-
forming the church.

Jesus could very well be saying, "Upon Ferguson,
Charleston, and Minneapolis—sites of some of the most notorious racial conflicts in our time—I will build my church."
Jesus is saying the church cannot be silent about what is happening in the culture. Instead, it must bring answers to the
problems that ail us—and for America, that especially means
speaking up about race.

But there's more. Notice Jesus says of the church that the
"gates of hell shall not prevail against it" (Matthew 16:18). We
don't have to spend a day in seminary or take a trip to Caesarea Philippi to get our arms around what Jesus is saying:
Gates guard. Gates protect. Gates don't play offense.

Gates play defense.

While the gates of hell are backpedaling, the church should
be fast-breaking. While the gates of hell are reacting, the
church should be initiating. The church Jesus envisions is a
church on the offensive. Yet when it comes to the issue of race,
hell is fast-breaking while we, the church, are backpedaling.

Until we learn to play offense by engaging in a robust discipleship in which followers of Jesus are being formed into a
new humanity, we will always find hell snapping at our heels.
I've seen it over and over again in my lifetime.

When Dylan Roof killed nine African Americans attending
midweek Bible study in a Charleston, South Carolina, church,
I was immediately hit up by well-meaning non–African
American followers of Jesus asking what they could do. What
books should they be reading? What should they say at their
churches the following Sunday? While it's hard for me to give
homework while I'm grieving, I relented. For the next several

days, our attention was riveted on the subject of race. But then the uproar died down, and as is the case in the news cycle, something else captured our collective concerns. Then another racial event inevitably happened, and the same questions of what to read, what to preach, and what to do flooded my direct messages. I responded, and then came Ahmaud Arbery. Everything stopped. People posted the runs they did in honor of Arbery and asked the same questions. We went back to life as we knew it. Then Breonna Taylor happened. Then George Floyd. Then . . .

And in the midst of all this came a report that the two most divided groups are White evangelicals and Blacks. How can this be when we've talked about race as much as we have? This happens when we are used to reacting and not leading, backpedaling and not fast breaking, playing defense when Christ has called us to play offense. This book contends that the church must play offense by demonstrating a paradigm of discipleship that is both vertical and horizontal, showing people how to walk with God and with each other.

Christianity is at odds with America's obsession with the individual, for Christianity contends that transformation happens within the context of relationships. How does God change us? By connecting us sinners with him and with others. This is the fabric of the great commandment and the essence of the Bible.

Korie and I have been married for several decades. One thing I've learned through our years together is the inevitability of change. Someone once quipped that his wife had been married to five different men and all of them had been him. Understanding this, my and Korie's conversation turned one evening to how we had changed. She observed that I have become much kinder and more compassionate. Because she is not at all given to flattery, I found her insights to be greatly encouraging and a true credit to both God and her. I was a completely different person on that late-nineties summer day when we said "I do" in a Southern California church. Words like *abrasive* and *sexist* were apt descriptors of me then. With great shame I admit the hurt I inflicted on my wife.

What interests me is how my transformation came about. We did go to some conferences and counseling sessions. And while those helped, I can say without hesitation that the most beneficial decision I made that led to my emerging kindness was to lean into close relationship with my wife.

As a man, I not only do not understand women, but I also carry deep biases in me that have manifested in patriarchal dispositions and are what Dr. Derald Wing Sue of Columbia University has popularized as "microaggressions." I am convinced my maturation in my treatment of women could not have happened without being in close, meaningful proximity with a woman I deeply loved and being committed to seeing her flourish.

The church that plays offense when it comes to race is the kind of church that will never settle for diversity but will be committed to ethnic unity, nurtured through a relentless commitment to having substantive relationships with the other. We all harbor our own racial biases, which manifest as microaggressions (dare I offer: at times, "*macro*aggressions"), causing deep hurt and even trauma to our ethnically other siblings. The only way forward is a commitment to a healthy, proactive, and relational offense that seeks to bridge the ethnic divide, is quick to engage in hard but necessary conversations, dives deep into humility by admitting the wrong and walking the road of repentance, and extends huge helpings of grace and forgiveness toward offenders—all in the hopes of emerging as the new humanity the church is to embody and model.

If transformation were boiled down to simply reading a book, God would have given us his Word, aborted the church, and said, "Read this and I'll see you in heaven." And God for sure would not have given us his Holy Spirit, whose very role is relational in guiding us and manifesting fruit in our lives, allowing us to be a blessing to those we come in contact with. The point is this: the Bible is essential, but so is its premise of Christians living in relationship with God and others. These relationships transform us from fleshly jerks filled with racial biases to a new humanity filled with love and empathy for others.

If you're a University of Alabama football fan, September 12, 1970, should mean something to you. Not because you won, but precisely because you lost. Rather, Alabama got blown out—by a University of Southern California (USC) football team with a Black quarterback and an all-Black backfield. Alabama's team was all White. Played in the Deep South, this game showed Alabama fans the value of people of color and what a multiethnic team looked like. It's said that USC played so well and beat 'Bama so thoroughly that they did more for the cause of racial justice in Alabama in that single night than Dr. King and the civil rights movement did in decades. That may be an overstatement—but when it came to race, USC played offense while 'Bama had played defense for years, and the result was a stunning 42–21 defeat for the Crimson Tide.

Almost immediately, Alabama's legendary coach, Paul "Bear" Bryant, began recruiting players of color. And while it pains me to say this as a University of Georgia fan, Alabama began winning many more championships than they had before. The culture of college football was changed, precisely because of a USC team that refused to be limited by the culture.

It's time for us to play offense. The enemy has been wearing us out for far too long. Let's lean into this new humanity that God has called us to.

ETHNIC UNITY DISCUSSION

We as the church play offense when we get into relationships with the ethnic other, which is easier said than done. What are some challenges people face when forming cross-ethnic relationships?

How have relationships with the ethnic other transformed you?

How might you encourage your church to play offense in the area of ethnic unity?

CHAPTER TWO

✝

SEEING THROUGH THE FOG

FLORENCE CHADWICK LOVED A CHALLENGE. Tell her she couldn't do something, and she was guaranteed to give it a try. She was the first woman to swim the English Channel back and forth. In 1952, she stepped into the waters just off the coast of Catalina Island seeking to become the first woman to swim from there to California. For over fifteen long and grueling hours, she braved the waters of the Pacific Ocean with her mother cheering her on in the boat beside her. Then Chadwick ran out of steam just one mile from the coast.

At the press conference afterward, she said, "All I could see was the fog. . . . I think if I could have seen the shore, I would have made it." Two months later, Chadwick returned to those same waters and completed her mission of becoming the first woman to swim from Catalina to California.[1]

Chadwick failed on her first try because she lacked vision. She lost sight of the destination. In many ways, I think this is the problem with both our culture and the church: we can't see the proverbial shore when it comes to matters of ethnic unity.

The church is meant to be the culture's desired destination. In other words, the people of God represent the shore to which culture should aspire to arrive, not the other way around. There should be something so compelling, so inspiring by how we relate to one another that it drives culture to check us out. We catch glimpses of this with the early church. Luke was careful to note the church's multiethnic and multicultural origins (Acts 2). He observed their devotion to one another, noting that this eclectic, Christ-saturated community was so committed to each other they sold their possessions and gave to those who were in need (Acts 2:45). He even pointed out several times they had "all things in common" (Acts 2:44; 4:32). At the same time, Luke documented the church's growth, as their numbers were increasing daily with thousands joining in a short span of time. What must not be lost in all of this is the connection between unity and church growth. Many in the culture were frantically making their way to the shoreline of the church, and what led the way was not just the gospel *proclaimed* but the gospel *practiced* through a vibrant, multiethnic, and multicultural community.

Culture is not breaking its neck to get to the shoreline of the church today. Even more disheartening are the many stories of people leaving the church because the fog of politics, racism, nationalism, and the like have blurred the beauty of the bride of Christ. You may even feel like Florence Chadwick as you read this. The church's failure to truly love has fatigued you. You're worn out by leaders who failed to speak boldly to issues of injustice. You're tired of crossing your fingers on the way to corporate worship, wishing someone would speak to the grief you and your ethnic kin are feeling, only to leave lamenting in isolation. Or maybe you're a leader exhausted by the constant pushback you get when you speak up and the complaints you get when you don't.

We need a fresh vision of the shoreline. But what exactly *is* the shoreline? Diversity is a great step, but it's not the destination: *unity* is. Jesus' final prayer before the cross was not for diversity but unity. In my years working with aspiring multiethnic churches, I've discovered ethnic diversity without ethnic unity ultimately results in ethnic homogeneity. When a multiethnic church stops at diversity, it will eventually lose groups of people. For a church to play offense, it must constantly fight for unity.

OUR TRUE IDENTITY

The church of Corinth and the church of Ephesus were both planted by Paul. Both churches were multiethnic. When Paul came to Corinth to establish the church there, he "tried to persuade Jews and Greeks" (Acts 18:4). One chapter later, we find Paul in Ephesus where he "continued for two years, so that all the residents of Asia heard the word of the Lord, both Jews and Greeks" (Acts 19:10). Both churches, though diverse, needed to be encouraged toward unity. But how did Paul go about this?

When I was a kid, my mother's medicine cabinet was pretty simple. Outside of a few Band-Aids, all I remember was a bottle of the dreaded cod liver oil. If you've never had cod liver oil, consider yourself blessed and highly favored. I haven't tasted anything more disgusting in my life. Seriously. I remember holding my breath as "Dr. Mom" administered it to me. She believed that it could solve whatever ailed us. Got the beginnings of a cold? Cod liver oil. Feeling a little fatigued? Cod liver oil. Feeling fine, but the weather is changing, which means you *might* get sick? Cod liver oil. Mama's approach to healing wasn't complicated. She took one thing and applied it to a host of problems.

Like my mother, Paul had a very simplistic approach to whatever was ailing the body of Christ—thankfully not cod liver oil, but the gospel. How did you deal with believers who were taking each other to court? The gospel. What did you do with divisions over food offered to idols? The gospel. And what about partiality being shown to rich believers during the Lord's Supper? The gospel. Paul illuminated the primacy of the gospel to bring about unity in the midst of division.

This is everything when we talk about the shoreline of ethnic unity in the church. While racism is a demonic system set up to extract value from people based on the color of their skin, the gospel says our value was firmly established at the moment of conception when we were created by a benevolent God in the image of God. That value only escalated when Jesus died in our place for our sins. My ultimate identity, therefore, is not found in my Blackness, and yours is not found in your being Korean, Colombian, or White. Yes, our ethnicity is a necessary, redemptive part of our story, but it is not *the* story.

This is easier said than lived out because our world consistently disciples us away from gospel identity into lesser identities like ethnicity. Some years ago while in Johannesburg, South Africa, my friends and I visited the Apartheid Museum. During apartheid, the South African government established four main groups of people: Native, Colored, Asian, and White, with each group assigned a card that marked their ethnicity. These cards determined where they could live, who they could marry, and where they could work. These cards became their identity.

I was looking forward to experiencing the museum with the White members of our group, but on entering, we were

given the apartheid identity cards and were immediately seg-
regated from one another. I had a visceral sense of loss when
I was separated from my friends. This of course was by design,
with the museum seeking to imitate the experience of millions of people during this tragic era.

Imagine you are a pastor in South Africa during this ugly
period of apartheid. You are looking out at a sea of Whites
who have been culturally formed to have an inflated view of
self based on their pigmentation. Or you are pastoring a
Black church in Soweto where the collective psyche of your
congregants has been traumatized into inferiority. What
does your preaching look like? Do you never speak to these
things? Are you content with the gates of hell running up the
score of cultural formation on your people? Or do you play
offense and counter the false narratives of the culture with
the true narrative of the gospel by reminding them their
identity is not in their ethnicity but in Christ?

Now apartheid has ended, and you are leading a multiethnic church of Natives, Coloreds, Asians, and Whites. Does
not the residue of misplaced ethnic identity still exist among
your people? Will decades of racism not leak out into your
assembly? The people no longer carry their identity cards, but
they are still emblazoned on their minds. It would be pastoral
malpractice and Christian malpractice to not counteract
these demonic voices with the voice of Calvary.

Beyond apartheid in South Africa, America has experienced racism for several hundred years—since its inception.
The seizing of Native lands, slavery, Jim Crow, Japanese in-
ternment camps, poor treatment of Latino migrant workers,
anti-Muslim profiling, and acts of violence against the Asian
community became normalized in America, and the trauma

did not end when the laws changed. To this day, we live in a country that forms us away from gospel identity into the lesser identity of race.

Paul and Tenisha Austin, a Black couple living in Marin City, California, recently had their home appraised. Feeling that the appraisal came back low, they decided to conduct an experiment. They took down all the pictures of themselves and any other Black people. Then they asked a White friend to stand in for them and pretend she was the owner of the house, a method commonly referred to as "whitewashing." Finally, they engaged a different appraiser. The result was a 50 percent increase in home value.[2] Merely asking someone White to pretend the home was hers added hundreds of thousands of dollars in value.

I do not say these things to guilt anyone, but if Paul and Tenisha come into a multiethnic church, they will understandably bring their suspicions with them. Racism has formed them. How do they become reformed? Silence is not an option. Nor is a Western paradigm of discipleship that stops at their vertical relationship with God. Instead, they need to see how the gospel comes to bear on their identity and relationships with others.

We have no hope of ethnic unity without gospel identity. This is Paul's point when he writes to another multiethnic church: the Ephesians. He pleads with them to walk in unity: "I therefore, a prisoner for the Lord, urge you to walk in a manner worthy of the calling to which you have been called, with all humility and gentleness, with patience, bearing with one another in love, eager to maintain the unity of the Spirit in the bond of peace" (Ephesians 4:1-3). Then he gives them the gospel, the foundation for their multiethnic unity: "There is one body and one Spirit—just as you were called to the one hope that belongs to your call—one Lord, one faith, one baptism, one God and Father of all" (Ephesians 4:4-6). Paul shows the Ephesians that gospel unity can only happen because of their gospel identity, which is anchored in the Trinity.

Gospel identity means God accepts us because of what Christ did for us on the cross. We are not accepted because we have behaved. We are not accepted because our parents or grandparents went to church. We are not accepted because of our skin color or economic status. We are not accepted because we refused to oppress. We are not accepted because we were, or are, oppressed. We are accepted—declared righteous by God—because of the righteousness of Christ that was imputed, or transferred, to our lives.

My children attend universities that cost more than they can afford. Yet they are able to have a relationship with the school, attend classes, learn from professors, and eat and sleep on campus not because of their resources, but because my wife and I have transferred financial resources from our accounts to theirs. In the same way, sin has left us a bill that we do not have the ability to pay. There is no amount of quiet time, tithing, or church attendance that can satisfy our debt. But you and I can have a relationship with Jesus and be adopted into the family of God because of the One who died in our place for our sins on the cross. This is the foundation of gospel identity.

However, gospel identity does not mean the eradication of ethnicity. Revelation 5 and 7 point out that heaven will be filled with people of every ethnicity. This is telling, because John's heavenly vision reveals ethnicity is not a fruit of the fall but rather a part of our future eternal reality. What this means for us now is that our *ethnos*, or ethnicity, is part of us being made in the image of God. And yet, Satan has done such a number on us that race has become a major hindrance to getting to the shoreline of ethnic unity.

THREATS TO ETHNIC UNITY: COLORBLINDNESS

There are two great threats to ethnic unity: colorblindness and ethnic idolatry. Gospel identity is not code for colorblindness, for several reasons. One is that the Scriptures teach a counternarrative to colorblindness. It really is amazing the many instances where the authors of the Bible point out ethnicity. Moses married an African woman. Jesus had a notorious conversation with a Samaritan woman at a well. Luke documents the impact of the gospel on an Ethiopian eunuch. And Paul, in Ephesians 2, transgresses the so-called ethic of colorblindness by talking about "Gentiles *in the flesh*" (Ephesians 2:11, emphasis mine). So, to be colorblind is to be at odds with the witness of Scripture.

Colorblindness pulls the rug out from any hopes of solidarity with the ethnic other. To get at this, we must understand one of the greatest threats to the early church was a false teaching called Gnosticism. This teaching, in asserting that the body was bad and the spirit was good, diminished the humanity of Christ. The apostle John took issue with the Gnostics right from the beginning of his first letter when he wrote of Jesus, "That which was from the beginning, which we have heard, which we have seen with our eyes, which we looked upon and have touched with our hands, concerning the word of life—the life was made manifest, and we have seen it, and testify to it and proclaim to you the eternal life, which was with the Father and was made manifest to us" (1 John 1:1-2).

Notice the very physical and sensory terms John uses to depict Jesus. He has heard Jesus, meaning there was a voice. He has seen, looked upon, and touched Jesus. Jesus has been made manifest. Oh, the physicality. Later, John points out the embodied Jesus enabled him to have "fellowship . . . with . . . Jesus Christ" (1 John 1:3). What John is saying has profound ramifications for our discussion on ethnic unity: Jesus came in embodied form, so to deny the humanity of Jesus is to hinder fellowship with him (1 John 1:1-10). In the same way, to deny the full humanity in others is to hinder fellowship with them.

Gnosticism still exists in evangelical circles today when it comes to race. We moan about having to hear messages on racism, even accusing our preachers and others of cultural Marxism and wokeness. We want to "just preach the gospel" and ignore the body. Focus on souls, not skin, is the worldview of many in the body of Christ. What can we call this other than modern Gnosticism?

Yet we are more than spirits; we are also embodied beings with what the Scriptures call *ethnos*, or ethnicity. There is a story that comes with my Blackness, your Whiteness, your Asian-ness, your Latino-ness, and so on. To be colorblind is to go the route of Gnosticism and ignore a major part of who we are. And when we ignore dimensions of people, we have no hope of ethnic unity, because unity means hearing each other's unabridged stories and coming to terms with truth.

In his book *The Loneliest Americans*, Korean writer Jay Caspian Kang pulls us into the Asian experience of trying to navigate the Black/White binary in America. He observes, "There is no meaningful, political way to deal with the pain and disappointment of being an Asian American, no answer for the exclusion you feel when everyone around you talks about racism and white supremacy and you know—at some visceral level—that you're not allowed to speak up. You are an ally, not a stakeholder."[3] How can one read these words by Kang and not feel what the Koreans call *jung*, which can best be described as empathy and obligation? As hard as these things may be to hear, we must hear them if we have any hope for ethnic unity. Colorblindness may be easier for some, but the only thing it can accomplish is a mirage of oneness.

THREATS TO ETHNIC UNITY: ETHNIC IDOLATRY

Ethnic idolatry does not foster an environment of ethnic unity, either. Many Christian leaders have defined idolatry as disordered loves and misplaced priorities. An idol is anything, even a good thing, that becomes an ultimate thing. Ethnicity is good, but when it is put first, it becomes disastrous. There are many faces or expressions of ethnic idolatry. Let me give you two.

One is the aggressive face of ethnic idolatry. We see this with domestic terrorist groups such as the KKK and even at various marches in recent memory. On a level down, but still as idolatrous, is the constant stream of video-documented incidents in which Whites have called the police on people of color they are convinced should not be in their neighborhood or holding a large cookout at a local park or bird-watching. In these incidents, an insidious form of aggressive racism conveys Whites are the insiders and people of color are the perpetual outsiders. This damages any aspirations of ethnic unity.

I once counseled a couple whose marriage was threatened by infidelity. The wife was naturally undone by her adulterous husband. When we finished the counseling session, I assumed she would exercise her biblical right to exit the marriage. A week or so later, I checked in to see how things were going. The husband informed me she had decided to delay any decision to see if there was repentance on his part. That meant every morning, before he got out of bed (they were separated), he had to record a video of himself on his phone saying he was a low-down dirty dog, unworthy of her love and affection, and send it to her.

Yes, the wife was victimized by her husband. And yes, the husband would have to walk the long, delicate road of reconciliation and be reminded that trust, though it can be broken in an instant, takes exponentially longer to repair. But if the wife decides to reconcile, she also has to make the decision to cease with his recordings. She will have to go to war with her identity as the oppressed while he goes to war with his identity as an oppressor. Both will have to rest in a greater identity of God's vision for marriage, which is oneness.

If you feel this is extreme, welcome to the state of race relations in America today. It is historic fact that people of color in America have been violated and betrayed by Whites for centuries. And now there is a movement afoot to make White people pull out their figurative phones and perpetually say how awful they are. While there must be confession and repentance for any relationship to move forward, at some point we must stop picking up our phones and move back in, navigating the awkwardness of the past while plodding toward reconciliation.

The great writer and pastor Eugene Peterson remarked that "words have ways of shaping us."[4] White supremacy, White fragility, and White privilege are all very real concepts that shape us in dehumanizing ways. Is repentance possible for a White supremacist? Is one allowed to ever genuinely confess without being canceled by their fellow ethnic siblings in Christ? Rick Warren pioneered Celebrate Recovery because he did not like the message of Alcoholics Anonymous that people were always defined by their vice. Can we not also "celebrate recovery" for those who are walking the forever road of repentance from racism? The gospel says yes. Ethnic idolatry says no.

And what happens when the church of Jesus Christ, which should represent the shoreline of ethnic unity, treats racism as if it is the unpardonable sin? The racists will keep their mouths shut and not speak up when the conversation turns to matters of ethnicity. One-way conversations, as we know, are not recipes for oneness.

But a more subtle and passive form of ethnic idolatry happens when my identity is placed in *my* scars and not *Christ's* scars. Sarah Shin observes, "The reality of the fall is that each of our cultures has experienced sin and evil. As a result, we can define our view of our ethnicity by its scars: I'm the sin, or I'm the sin done to me. And our view of other ethnicities can also be to define it by its scars."[5]

I see a growing problem among people of color trying to navigate spaces predominately occupied by our White evangelical siblings. When ethnic individuals who become followers of Jesus are discipled in an exclusively vertical trajectory (just them and God) in one of these environments, they inevitably assimilate to both the content and cultural context in which Jesus was presented to them. Given the pervasive nature of sin, it is only a matter of time before they are exposed to some racially insensitive event that jolts them out of their assimilation. What then transpires is an overreach, where in an attempt to medicate their ethnic wound, they form an identity based on their scars. Everything now becomes about race. Suspicion is automatic, and they refuse to believe the best in others. Bitterness and anger become constant companions. I am not saying there's no place for anger or lament. However, indifference and cynicism are of no help in the work of reconciliation.

I know firsthand the problem with forming one's identity around the trauma of racism. As a college student at a White evangelical school, I was devastated when a White classmate called me a racially charged name and the school did nothing to reprimand him. I have been discriminated against when it comes to housing, had White elders abuse their power by demanding things from me in an unjust manner, been called a "n_____" on the golf course (in progressive California of all places), and been pulled over by White cops who made me lie face down on the asphalt all because I was young and driving my pastor's luxury car. And these are just a few of many incidents.

So how does one cope in the midst of such trauma? My temptation has been to participate in the "Woke Olympics"—not for the sake of raising awareness of a real issue but to prove to myself I am indeed redemptively Black. This led me to lash out and cancel White people, even in the name of the gospel, to feel better about my embodied self. I often delivered my pain-induced outbursts with a Bible in hand while standing on some stage talking to a majority White audience. I either was dismissed or ended up producing guilt-driven Whites who then sought atonement for their sins, not in the finished work of Jesus Christ but in their own moral strivings.

So we didn't arrive at the shoreline of ethnic unity, but the scar tissue of my misplaced identity gave birth to Whites who likewise misplaced their identity. This works in a million different directions. When any person bases their ultimate identity around their ethnicity, and particularly the scars of their ethnicity, it sets off a chain reaction that makes ethnic unity impossible.

CHRIST'S SCARS, NOT MY SCARS

We are in need of a higher identity. Unity is only possible when we strive for something beyond us to bring us together. Examples of this abound. In the world of team sports, players do not step onto the court or field doing whatever they want. Instead, they adhere to a playbook. No matter how talented individual musicians are, they must each submit to the music already laid out for them in order to play beautiful music at a symphony.

What the playbook is to the athlete, or sheet music to a musician in the symphony, the gospel is to followers of Jesus. I am not advocating amnesia of one's pain and suffering. Miroslav Volf says, "One should never demand of those who have suffered wrong that they 'forget' and move on. This impossible advice would be also the wrong advice."[6] Award-winning writer and survivor of the Nazi death camps Elie Wiesel continues Volf's line of thinking. Drawing from his own racial trauma, Wiesel reflects, "We remember Auschwitz and all that it symbolizes because we believe that, in spite of the past and its horrors, the world is worthy of salvation; and salvation, like redemption, can be found only in memory."[7] Remembering the pain one has experienced, and even the pain one has inflicted, can bring redemptive good to our world. People like Fannie Lou Hamer, John Perkins, and a host of others engaged in the work of justice and reconciliation trace the tributaries of their labors back to the river of racial pain and suffering, and the result is a better world.

So, the gospel is not a call to forget our pain and suffering. Nor is it an invitation to dismiss our ethnicity. But when I, as a Black man, choose to locate my identity in the scars of Jesus, I must ask, "Who are those scars for?" I am brought to the conclusion that no one people group has a monopoly on those scars. Jesus died for the world. Jesus died for oppressed Jews as well as Roman centurions. Calvary dismantles the oppressed/oppressor binary.

Jesus' scars have something profound to say to those in power as well. He showed a special proclivity for the marginalized. In his last sermon before the cross, Jesus announced he so related to the downcast that our acts of altruism toward the incarcerated, the sick, and the homeless are actually done to him. Listen to his teaching, and you will find dire warnings of what awaits people who mistreat the poor. Therefore, having one's identity in the scars of Jesus is a Christ-centered concern, dare I even say sacrificial sympathy, for the least of these. Racism, classism, misogyny, and any other kind of abuse of power or discrimination are so out of step with the gospel, one would be right to question a person's salvation.

And yet, we must remember the premise of this book: the church of Jesus Christ continues to play defense and not offense because of our failure to offer a robust discipleship vision, which entails both a vertical and horizontal framework in which people are connected relationally to God and one another, especially the ethnic other. Any kind of gospel that does not attempt to bring about restorative relationships is a false gospel incongruent with the life of Christ and teachings of Scripture. We have union with God and with one another because of the scars of Christ. We are together a people of the scars of Christ.

The civil rights icon John Lewis is an example of this. At an early age he became a follower of Jesus and sensed God was calling him to ministry. A few years later, Lewis left for college to prepare for the pastorate. While enrolled in school, he became engaged in the civil rights movement and embraced the philosophy of nonviolent resistance. And in 1961 at the age of twenty-one, John Lewis became a Freedom Rider, seeking to integrate bus terminals across the South.

One of the Freedom Riders' stops was Rock Hill, South Carolina, where an angry mob of Whites awaited them. Not long after stepping off the bus, Lewis was assaulted by a man named Elwin Wilson. While being attacked, Lewis reverted to his training in nonviolent resistance. He curled up so his internal organs would escape direct blows and remembered it was not enough to simply endure the beating or to resist the urge to strike back. Rather, he had been trained to actively love the person who was hitting him.[8] The beating left him "woozy and feeling stabs of sharp pain above both eyes and in my ribs. My lower lip was bleeding pretty heavily."[9] Finally, Wilson was called off by a police officer who had a front row seat to the violence and had waited until he was ready to intervene. Lewis declined to press charges, and though he needed a doctor, he refused to go without first having a cup of coffee.

Lest you think this is just another nauseating historical account of a beating from that era, you should know Elwin Wilson could not get out of his mind the man who refused to fight back and instead chose to actively love. For decades, both his and John Lewis's actions haunted him. Eventually, Wilson placed his faith and identity in Jesus. And then the unthinkable—in 2009, almost fifty years after his vicious assault on Lewis—Elwin reached out to John for forgiveness. Not only did John forgive him, but the two went on to speak together on the power of forgiveness and reconciliation.

What brings a violent, hate-filled White man to ask forgiveness from his victim? The gospel. What enables the receiver of such hate to forgive? One who has placed his identity not in his scars but in *his* scars. And what brings about reconciliation and ethnic unity? Gospel identity, a kind that John lived out in 1961.

INDICATOR LIGHTS OF GOSPEL IDENTITY

Gospel identity is not so much a box to be checked as a moment-by-moment decision to be made. All sin is the refusal to find our identity and contentment in Christ. So how do we know if we are walking in gospel identity and setting the stage for ethnic unity? Let me offer two indicator lights of gospel identity.

One is forgiveness. Unforgiveness is idolatry because it reveals I treasured what I was wounded over more than I treasure Christ. That's a lot to take in, but it's important to understand that forgiveness and reconciliation are two different things. You can forgive without being reconciled, but it's impossible to be reconciled without forgiving. Let us remember ethnic unity is reconciliation, and without forgiveness, ethnic unity is impossible. Reconciliation is a desired goal, but because it takes two parties, it may or may not happen, which is why Paul tells the Romans to do their best to be at peace with all people (Romans 12:18). This verse is helpful because it tells me there are times reconciliation just doesn't happen even when I do my best. But there are no loopholes when it comes to forgiveness, because forgiveness takes one. So what am I saying when I refuse to forgive even though I know Christ requires me to forgive? Well, I am choosing to hold on to the thing I was hurt by more than I am holding on to Christ, which exposes my idol.

Earlier, I shared about the time I was called a racially insensitive word in college. This incident spiked my anger, and over time, my decision not to forgive grew a root of bitterness in me. This not only hindered my relationship with this specific individual but also distorted my view of a whole group of people. I didn't realize at the time that I had chosen to redirect my identity from Christ to my own scars. I had exchanged gospel identity for ethnic identity. And while there is room for both, only one can be first. Conversely, when I finally made the decision to forgive, I was saying through my act of releasing the offense that I was elevating Christ to his number one ranking in my life. No, the act of forgiveness doesn't immediately remove the hurt, but it makes ethnic unity possible. Who do you need to forgive? What Elwin Wilson (no matter their color or gender) has wounded you, and you need to release the offense, making ethnic unity possible?

Another indicator light of gospel identity is sympathy, which at its core means to suffer with. The writer of the book of Hebrews tells us we have, in Christ, a high priest who can sympathize with our weaknesses (Hebrews 4:15). As our advocate, Jesus is able to plead on our behalf because he can relate to our struggle, having been "tempted as we are, yet without sin" (Hebrews 4:15). Where did such deep-seated sympathy come from? Jesus left the comforts of heaven, took on flesh, and enmeshed himself in the narrative of humanity. He came as an ethnic minority, a Jew. He showed unusual, culture-defying honor to women—sitting with them at a well, forgiving one who was caught in adultery while standing up to her accusers, and allowing himself to be misunderstood by the religious elite when a sinful woman came weeping literally at his feet. Jesus' sympathy, the writer of Hebrews indicates, is connected to his proximity to the human condition.

We know we are walking in gospel identity when we refuse to dismiss people's racial pain and travails and take time to sit at the proverbial well with the ethnic other. This sympathy only grows as we become relationally connected in true fellowship with an ethnically eclectic community. This is why dismissing a person as being a liberal or woke or a cultural Marxist because they simply want to have the conversation goes against the grain of gospel identity and fails to display Christlike sympathy. Sure, we need to be committed to truth and admonish people when they are clearly in error, yet to not even listen to people's stories is one of the most non-Christlike things we can do.

When we were little, we learned the alphabet song. You know how it goes. In fact, you're probably humming it. Now try singing the song without starting with the letter *A*. Doesn't quite work, does it?

As we swim to the shoreline of ethnic unity, gospel identity is our letter *A*. Without it, ethnic unity doesn't quite work.

ETHNIC UNITY DISCUSSION

There's a difference between ethnic diversity and ethnic unity. In fact, ethnic diversity without ethnic unity is harmful. What do you think of this statement? What are some examples of the harm that comes from diversity without unity that you have personally experienced?

Ethnic unity begins with gospel identity. How might you practically live into this daily?

How can your church champion a culture that celebrates ethnic diversity instead of being colorblind?

How have you seen ethnic idolatry among the people of God? How can the church challenge it in a way that doesn't swing to colorblindness?

CHAPTER THREE

✝

COMMUNAL IDENTITY
AND ETHNIC UNITY

"WHAT HAPPENS TO ME WHEN I DIE?" is one of the great questions of life. Most of us ask this as it pertains to both our soul and our body; the Romans certainly did. In the world in which Christianity was birthed, dying without a proper burial was one of people's worst fears. If this happened to you, you were left to the elements or wild beasts. And in a culture where family and legacy were everything, this was especially problematic.

To help alleviate these fears, businesses called funerary unions arose, where people paid a monthly fee to guarantee a decent burial. The only problem was that it was set up for people of means, not for people who were poor. Therefore, the normal Roman cemetery, called the catacombs, was dominated by the affluent. On the occasion that the poor were buried among the wealthy, a boundary marker such as a fence or a wall was erected between the two. Even in death, segregation was a value. Followers of Jesus would soon change all of this.

The Catacomb of Priscilla in Rome, for example, offers a helpful counternarrative. The burial system had no boundaries separating the rich from the poor. Archaeologist John Bodel points out,

> The novelty in the catacombs is that the two forms of burial (rich and poor) are integrated with each other and housed within the same undefined space. [What we see is] a heterogeneous mixture of persons of different wealth and status with no distinctively unifying beliefs about the representation of privilege in burial. [A Christian catacomb was thus] a world of its own, without normal parameters.[1]

In life and death, followers of Jesus were unflinching in their commitment to play offense, which was seen in their transcultural unity.

CULTURAL SCRIPTS

The people buried in these catacombs were handed a cultural script from the moment they were born. A cultural script is a way of seeing, living in, and navigating the world, informed by a host of factors such as language, ethnicity, class, and locale. Long before apartheid riddled South Africa, Rome had its own figurative identity cards, which formed an immutable caste system that made unity for most people either undesirable or so unbelievable they couldn't imagine it. What changed these people from lives tethered to their places in society to shaking their fists in "heterogeneous mixture" in burial? The church.

Like those in the ancient Roman world, we all have been handed cultural scripts—cues from our families of origin and culture that feed the way we navigate others and our world. You have them, and so do I.

Some years ago, I preached at a church where I am really good friends with a few of the pastors. A few hours before the service, I was at their apartment when one of my friends emerged from the bathroom with what looked like a plastic grocery bag. I watched him take this bag outside across the parking lot to the dumpster. When he came back, I asked him why he did that. He gave me a curious look and said this is what he always does when he gets out of the bathroom. I returned his look and told him that's what the toilet is for. I later found out he grew up poor and in a large family. When he was young, they went through a season where the toilet was always getting clogged. Instead of spending money they didn't have to fix it, his family threw out the toilet paper instead of flushing it. Here we were a few decades later, and he did this without thinking. His actions were on autopilot because of his cultural script. I hope our conversation that day eventually set him free!

Toilet paper aside, many of our cultural scripts are not as humorous. Not long after landing in Memphis, Tennessee, to plant a church we hoped would be multiethnic, our team found ourselves at Zion Cemetery, the oldest all-Black cemetery in the Mid-South. Zion Cemetery is a reminder of the institution of segregation, where even in death, the dividing line between Blacks and Whites was fixed. Originally, this burial ground was under the care of what was then known as the Colored Methodist Episcopal Church (now the Christian Methodist Episcopal Church), but due to financial constraints, the denomination was no longer able to provide the care these grounds required. Old abandoned cars, drug paraphernalia, and a plot of land overrun by weeds reminded me how far I was from the catacombs of Rome and cemented the sad reality that even in death, African Americans of the Jim Crow South were still treated as second class citizens. Their cultural scripts informed both their living and their dying.

For budding church planters, diversity is wonderful to fantasize about until you realize the hardest stretch to the shoreline of unity is from diversity to ethnic unity. What makes this road so arduous is the variety of cultural scripts in the room.

My assistant, Sharon, is Korean American. She once showed me a picture of her and her family dressed up in very vibrant colors and traditional Korean garb. Sharon explained that Lunar New Year is such a huge deal in the Korean community that the children even bring their parents money. It's their cultural script of showing honor.

I can relate to this as a Black man—not the taking money to my folks part, although I do think I'll institute that with my kids. The Black community has always been big on respect for authority. A lot of this was forged out of slavery and Jim Crow, when one wayward glance or a failure to address a White person by the proper title could get a Black person lynched. We had no margin for error. As a result, Black parents were forced to come down particularly hard on their children. Yelling and spanking often became reflex reactions as opposed to listening and talking. Like our Asian siblings, we in the Black community hold those in authority in high regard.

Black, brown, and Asian people also tend to be more communal. I am not saying White people do not desire community or relationships. The desire to know and be known is part of what it means to be image bearers. By communal, I mean a relational solidarity with one's ethnicity. I'm not attaching any sense of moral value when I say our White siblings do not have this kind of ethnic solidarity with their fellow Whites. Of course, I'm painting with a broad brush, but when White Americans reflect on the ugly history of slavery in our country, they tend to be careful to not say things like, "We owned slaves," or "We lynched." Instead, they tend to put as much distance as possible between their forefathers' actions and their own. Even today, when a White person is assaulted or becomes the victim of some injustice, other Whites are not coming to church the next Sunday hoping their pastor says something. It's not that they don't care; it's simply that their individualistic worldview doesn't naturally lend itself toward communal solidarity. On the other hand, their cultural script of individualism creates the worldview that if one could just work hard enough and assume responsibility for one's choices, achievement at the highest level is attainable.

Now imagine all these people with different cultural scripts sitting next to one another in church. How do you handle reparations? Do you avoid the conversation because it will offend one group of people whose cultural script knows nothing of communal culpability based on their ethnicity? What about our Asian siblings, whose value of honoring authority makes it difficult for them to express to their leadership how they are feeling about the many incidents of Asian-directed hate during the Covid-19 pandemic? If you as a leader do not understand our Asian kin, you might mistake their silence for them being okay.

And then there are other matters that may seem insignificant but are not—like small group events in a multiethnic context. When our family would plan barbecues at our home for, say, 2:30 in the afternoon and the doorbell rang exactly at 2:30, our young children would immediately say, "It has to be a White person." When the doorbell rang at 3:30, they would say it was a Black person. Rarely were they wrong. Some people value time, others value the event. My people may not get there on time, but believe me, they will have a good time and will practically need to be kicked out. (I can't tell you on how many occasions I've quoted the venerable godfather of soul, James Brown, to my beautiful Black brothers and sisters when I was ready to go to bed: "Y'all ain't got to go home, but you got to get out of here.") We have no hope of reaching the shoreline of ethnic unity until we see the scripts our people are holding.

One gets a sense of the early Christians' varied cultural scripts when walking their burial grounds. The burial inscriptions in the Roman catacombs unearth followers of Jesus from all walks of life. Scholar John Dickson says these cemeteries contained "a surprising array of occupations for believers: . . . artisans, tradesmen, minor civic officials, women silk weavers and horse-groomers," to name a few. One of the most fascinating epitaphs reveals a Christian comedian who had etched on his tomb, "From jokes I gained a handsome house and income . . . O death, you do not appreciate jokes."[2] Blue collar and white collar. Wealthy and poor. No boundaries. All together in a final earthly display of ethnic and cultural unity. But why? The early Christian thinker Lactantius explained that the Christian belief in the image of God led them to see their "last and greatest duty of piety" as making sure every believer had a proper burial together with other believers, no matter their ethnicity or culture.[3] And where did they learn of the image of God? In church where they sat next to artisans, tradesmen, and even comedians.

Socialization is essential to moving from diversity to unity. Robert P. Jones, the CEO and founder of The Public Religion Research Institute, observes that social segregation has wreaked havoc on race relations in America. And while there is nothing new in his analysis, what he says next is unsettling: "The overwhelming majority of white Americans don't have a single close relationship with a person who isn't white. . . . *There are virtually no American institutions positioned to resolve these persistent problems of systemic and social segregation.*"[4] But wait a minute, what about the church?

Relationships with the other is a vital ingredient to our growth. I once had an African American member who harbored suspicions of Whites birthed out of real pain. When he and his family first began to attend our multiethnic church, he was a bit standoffish, but over time his guard began to fall. He joined a small group that happened to be hosted at a White person's home. After a substantial period of time with this group, he shared with me that, even though he had grown up in this city, it wasn't until he came to our church that he was invited to a White person's home for the first time. He was forty-three. My friend's journey into a new humanity began only when he chose to be in proximity with the ethnic other, within a community of Christ-followers fiercely committed to unity.

Paul's vision of the church encompassed more than saving souls. Need I remind us many slave masters in the Antebellum South saw themselves as countercultural because they allowed "their property" to be preached to. Paul was after the establishment of an "institution" that would bring comprehensive reformation to the soul, the body, and relationships. This is why his appeal for unity to the multiethnic church at Ephesus deserves a return:

> I therefore, a prisoner for the Lord, urge you to walk in
> a manner worthy of the calling to which you have been
> called, with all humility and gentleness, with patience,

bearing with one another in love, eager to maintain the unity of the Spirit in the bond of peace. There is one body and one Spirit—just as you were called to the one hope that belongs to your call— one Lord, one faith, one baptism, one God and Father of all, who is over all and through all and in all. (Ephesians 4:1-6)

UNITY IS NOT UNIFORMITY

In the West, our default is to read the Bible as if it has to do solely with me, the individual. While there are secondary applications that focus on you or me, such as the Epistles, we should keep in mind that the Bible was mostly written to churches: a body of people. This leads to the question, *What kind of people are hearing this message?* As we learned in the last chapter, the church at Ephesus is multiethnic. In Ephesians 6, Paul takes the time to address servants and masters. In the passage above, we get just a hint at diversity. Paul uses words like *humility, gentleness,* and *patience.* These terms do not only imply sin but also point to a community with diversity of thought. I do not need to be patient with people who see things the way I do. Gentleness is most visible when I am at odds with someone. And humility has to do with showing deference to someone else. All these terms display a church that is a thorough mixture of rich and poor, men and women, Jew and Gentile—a place rife with various cultural scripts. In the middle of all the diversity, Paul makes an appeal for unity, not uniformity.

Some of us may remember a picture of a dress that took the world by storm in 2015.[5] The issue was not who made the dress or whether we felt it was beautiful. The central question had to do with the color of the dress. Millions of people offered very strong opinions via social media. Some said it was gold and white, others said it was black and blue. All of us were left wondering how we could look at the same thing and reach such drastically different conclusions.

We really do see things differently, and what often colors our perceptions of the world is our cultural script. No further proof is needed than the realm of politics. Election season in a multiethnic church can be a real headache. Politics is a sport played by the subjective, where one's economic status, set of experiences, relationships, and a host of other factors all come to bear at the ballot box. If Paul were writing to the church of America today, he would offer very little, if anything, as it relates to how we vote; instead, he would offer much on how we should relate to one another while we vote. Paul's calls for humility, gentleness, and patience are as needed now as they were then.

If the politics example hits a little too close to home, please know this is my intent. Politics within the Christian community is a prime example of the crucial idea that uniformity is not unity. Dr. Korie Edwards, professor of sociology at Ohio State University, once observed that, in a multiethnic setting, minorities look to Whites for permission on what is acceptable.[6] Conservative White evangelicals tend to vote Republican and harbor very strong opinions regarding the Democratic Party and its position on abortion. Without getting into the weeds, what is often missing from these political diatribes is nuance. Couple these strong political opinions with the strand of race, and you have a recipe for the veneer of unity, also known as uniformity. Minorities in multiethnic churches tend to be silent on these matters when they come up, feigning unity. This kind of silence is indicative of a lack of trust.

Please do not misunderstand me. I am not advocating for a verbal riot within our churches the next election cycle. Let us remember that Paul's choice of words—humility, gentleness, and patience—implies an atmosphere of free and responsible discourse, where variant viewpoints are expressed within a loving environment. It is an irrevocable principle of life: the more secure a person feels in a relationship, the more apt they are to disclose how they truly feel.

My mentor says it's not a relationship until the two of you scream at each other. Paul's admonition for humility, gentleness, and patience aside, my mentor has a point. Intimacy is never seen in a perpetual ceasefire where both sides choose outward compliance. Let's face it: if two people never argue, fuss, or fight and agree on every single thing, one of them is not necessary. The most textured and meaningful relationships are those in which both sides feel so safe with one another that they are free to "go there," even if it means offering variant points of view, because they know the MVP of all virtues—love—will keep the relationship intact.

Likewise, if I were to sit in your diverse small group for a significant period and observe there is only one dominant opinion on politics, women's roles in the church, and how to handle policing in our society, I would conclude you may have ethnic diversity but not ethnic unity. Diversity of faces without diversity of voices is a seditious kind of uniformity that wreaks havoc on the image of God.

These conversations are difficult to engage in, so we avoid them, mainly because we see no way to agree on the outcome. But to Jesus, Paul, and the church leaders, the outcome—or shoreline if you will—was not agreement on a particular issue, but unity. This leads us to assume unity can only be attained if we avoid certain issues, but this is patently false. Rather, when we circumvent divisive issues, we often circumvent community.

This is exactly what made the Truth and Reconciliation Commission in post-apartheid South Africa so meaningful. Sure, they could have said legislated segregation is over and moved on, but they understood there could be no hope of authentic relationships across ethnic lines until they decided to "go there" and "scream" at each other. This is the hard work of unity. Uniformity is content with skirting the topic; unity requires a peculiar kind of courage to wade into the discomfort.

Can we say we are walking in ethnic unity when our church never preaches on race, and even when the pastor does, it's so "balanced" nothing is really said? Are we really experiencing unity when we never discourse across the ethnic divide as to why so many conservative White evangelicals voted for Trump and why so many Blacks were offended? And can we say we are ethnically unified when people who are not a part of the Black/White binary refuse to say anything because they don't want to pick a side? While moments of silence may be wise at times, silence as a theme when it comes to race is not unity but uniformity. So how do we break free from uniformity and venture into unity?

UNION WITH CHRISTIANS DEMANDS UNION WITH CHRIST

In 1959, six men walked into Columbia Studios to record a jazz album. The group, led by the enigmatic Miles Davis, was a multiethnic ensemble, composed of jazz legends such as John Coltrane, Cannonball Adderley, and the White pianist Bill Evans. Working with this much talent would be a challenge. So how did Davis lead them during what would become a defining moment in the history of jazz? Poet and jazz historian Quincy Troupe observed that Davis's leadership style was to assemble the best talent and scribble each of their parts on scraps of paper. Those scraps contained the basic structure of the song, a structure they all agreed to adhere to. Yet at the same time, these men had the freedom to express their individuality through a medium that was all about improvisation. When the recording sessions concluded, the world was gifted with the number one selling jazz album of all time, *Kind of Blue*.[7] Produced in the era of bebop, *Kind of Blue* was unique because of its commitment to simplicity and freedom. These six men had agreed to a core set of notes that guided their playing, without losing who they were in the process.

At the center of Christian unity is a small "scrap of paper" known as the gospel, and the nucleus of the gospel is Jesus. When pressed on what life in the kingdom was all about, Jesus offered only two thoughts, which could fit on one of those scraps of paper Miles Davis handed his sextet: love for God and love for people. Apprenticeship to Jesus Christ—living the way he lived—is nothing more, nothing less.

When we commit ourselves to loving God with the totality of our being and loving others as ourselves, we are poised to experience ethnic unity. And yet, I hope you see what ethnic unity requires: commitment to an ethic higher than ethnicity. In other words, the best thing we bring to the table of ethnic unity is not our unique ethnic selves, as important as that may be, but our relationship with Jesus. Done right, the church of Jesus Christ, and not a liberal or progressive ideology based on the low ethic of tolerance, offers the purest picture of ethnic unity.

Like with any marriage, Korie and I are called to a distilled form of unity, a kind the Scriptures call oneness. But we are so different. We have gender differences, ethnic differences, family of origin differences, and so on. Over the years we've developed a snarky little saying when we sense the other is not in the best of moods. One of us will simply look at the other and say, "I see someone hasn't had their time with the Lord today." Not helpful, I know, but you see the sentiment behind the sarcasm. We are agreeing that what makes our marriage, our strivings toward oneness, attainable is our appeal to a scrap of paper beyond our cultural scripts—the gospel.

The best thing we offer any relationship is our walk with Jesus. This is exactly Paul's point to the Ephesians when, not long after his plea for unity, he redirects their attention upward to the Godhead, noting, "one Lord, one faith, one baptism, one God and Father of all, who is over all and through all and in all" (Ephesians 4:5-6). Like any cell phone needs to tap into a signal outside of itself to experience relationship with other phones, unity works because of our commitment to something beyond ourselves, which is Jesus and his glorious gospel.

In John 17, Jesus' final prayer before the cross focuses on unity. His prayer ends a section in John's Gospel known as the Upper Room Discourse, which begins in John 13. In the middle of Jesus' discourse, he commands his followers to abide in him (John 15). Before he gets to unity with others (John 17), he first discusses union with him. Jesus is saying we have no hope for right relationships with other people if we do not have a right relationship with him. Union with people demands union with Christ.

When it comes to drinking hot tea, there are two types of people: dippers and steepers. Dippers take the bag in and out of the hot water a few times before drinking. Steepers, on the other hand, let the tea bag stay in the water for a prolonged period, sometimes even while they enjoy their tea. What Jesus calls us to in John 15 is not to a life of inconsistent relational dipping with him, but to a life of steeping. The very word he uses for *abide*, in the original language, means to remain. When we remain in Jesus and do not dip in and out, we are poised for fruitfulness. Jesus says, "Whoever abides in me and I in him, he it is that bears much fruit, for apart from me you can do nothing" (John 15:5).

Paul may have had Jesus' words in mind when he wrote to the Galatians of the fruit of the Spirit (Galatians 5:22-23). Fruit exists to enhance others' lives. An apple tree does not exist for itself but for others. What is true in the natural world is also true in the spiritual. Many spiritual directors have rightly observed the telos of spiritual formation is not the individual; rather, Christ is formed in the person to better those around them. I am bettered so those around me are bettered.

This idea of bettered relationships through the individual's commitment to abide in Christ is further illumined by how Paul describes life in the flesh in Galatians 5. He is concerned not with skin and bone but with the antithesis of the Spirit—a life where the individual is in control and has abdicated their commitment to the gospel. He then names fifteen traits of what life in the flesh looks like, with over half of the list being relational chaos: "Now the works of the flesh are evident: sexual immorality, impurity, sensuality, idolatry, sorcery, *enmity, strife, jealousy, fits of anger, rivalries, dissensions, divisions, envy,* drunkenness, orgies, and things like these. I warn you, as I warned you before, that those who do such things will not inherit the kingdom of God" (Galatians 5:19-21, emphasis mine). The juxtaposition could not be any clearer. While the fruit of an abiding life in Christ enhances relationships, a life that refuses to abide in Christ and follow the Spirit erodes relationships. The implications of Paul's instructions are profound as it pertains to the church playing offense to achieve ethnic unity. He is saying we have no hope for ethnic unity if we do not abide in Jesus and walk in the power of the Spirit.

Of course, walking in the Spirit and abiding in Christ do not preclude one from disagreements with others. From birth, we have all been shaped by the various cultural scripts handed to us. A primary way God transforms us is by placing us in relationship with others who have very different ethnic and cultural views. Relational conflict is unavoidable, and I would even argue it's a sign of health. The Spirit helps us to navigate and emerge from these conflicts more like Christ.

Has much of the ethnic disunity we see in the church arisen from lives dominated by the flesh and not by the Spirit? The reflex response of calling people cultural Marxists or critical race theorists, instead of first trying to empathize and understand each other, indicates the flesh is in control and not the Spirit. Sending emails laced with unkind language runs counter to what Paul describes as life in the Spirit. And the cancel culture that's flooding the church is the very antithesis of Jesus' teaching on forgiveness and Paul's pleas for patience—an attribute of a person whose life is surrendered to the Spirit and not the flesh. The work of ethnic unity cannot be done under the influence of the flesh; instead, we must be intoxicated by the Spirit.

Life in the Spirit is essential to a community that aspires to walk in ethnic unity. In his classic *Mere Christianity*, C. S. Lewis argues the sin beneath all sins is pride, or what we might call life in the flesh. Pride, Lewis continues, needs comparison and competition in order to exist. In other words, for a person to feel good about themselves, they need those they regard as "less than" to exist. If all homes looked the same and held the same value, where would be my pride in my home? If all schools offered the same quality of education, where would my pride be in the school I attend? And if there was never a system in which a hierarchy of value was established based on the color of a person's skin, where is the pride in being White?

Lewis's argument holds special importance for our journey into ethnic unity. If Lewis is indeed right that all roads lead back to pride, then unforgiveness and vengeance are a face of pride. The choice to not release the wrongdoer of their offense is the wounded's attempt to inflict harm on the one who hurt them. Yet, as we know, this is a self-inflicted wound, making both healing and reconciliation impossible. It is a prideful attempt to even the score.

In the aftermath of George Floyd, I consulted with many churches experiencing a not-so-quiet exodus among people of color who, in their pain, felt that the leadership of their aspiring multiethnic assembly had not stewarded their power to advocate and care for the marginalized. Sadly, in my experience, there are far too many instances where this has happened, leaving people of color with no other choice than to advocate for themselves and protect their sense of emotional, mental, and spiritual well-being. What's more, just because a church is multiethnic does not mean there is an equitable distribution of power among all the groups represented. So, when racial trauma happens, those who have good reason to feel their voice is not as heard as other groups within the church quietly look for the exits without saying a word. All of these and more are factors that should help the leadership of aspiring multi-ethnic churches create safe environments where everyone feels heard, no matter their ethnicity, gender, or socioeconomic status. On the other hand, minorities should not have to look to our White siblings for permission to tell the truth. Isn't it ironic that those who feel powerless need to look to the powerful to speak, thus enabling the cycle of hurt and trauma?

One of the best things minorities can do is to be filled with the Spirit of God, stand in the power that is inherently theirs as children of God, and speak their minds with humility and gentleness. When both sides roll up their sleeves and do the work of creating safe, equitable environments, along with speaking truth in a way that is full of the Spirit and honors others' humanity, we are well on our way to breaking the cycle of ethnic disunity.

Paul's encouragement to the church at Ephesus to be "eager to maintain the unity of the Spirit" suggests an environment where unity is never a box to be checked but an ideal to be fought for. Just as a landscaper tends to the grass at someone's home each week, unity demands consistent cultivation. One of the greatest enemies of this spiritual landscaping work is timidity, because a timid person will not tend to the relational weeds that stifle the work of ethnic unity. It may shock you to know timid people are not humble. They shy away from conflict, worried that if the person they have an issue with really knew how they felt, that person wouldn't like them. Those who are timid have exchanged the health and potential maturity of the person they are in conflict with for themselves. Yes, James Baldwin, we hear you that to be a Black person and relatively conscious is to be in a state of rage all the time. But the Scriptures call us to give appropriate voice to that rage and not just leave the table of fellowship.

Lest you think I'm picking on minorities, remember our White siblings are also composed of pride and the flesh, which damage ethnic unity. Laura Ingraham's admonition to Lebron James to just "shut up and dribble" expresses the sentiments of so many conservative White evangelicals who desire to merely hear a gospel that deals with a person's soul, without confronting social inequities. Whenever I preach on or reference race in my sermons, I get a version of "shut up and dribble" in the many emails I receive and even from those who get up and leave mid-sermon.

This collective dismissal of pain and suffering is also a face of pride, because the messaging is one of comfort. People do not want to be reminded nor have it implied in any way they were connected to such suffering. And yet, Yale professor Miroslav Volf says such remembering is essential to a community's journey to the shoreline of ethnic unity:

> Remembering suffering awakens us from the slumber of indifference and goads us to fight against the suffering and oppression around us. . . . To struggle against evil, we must empathize with its victims. And to empathize with victims, we must know either from experience or from witnesses' stories what it means to hunger, thirst, shiver, bleed, grieve, or tremble in fear. The memory of past horror will make us loathe to tolerate it in the present.[8]

Volf is inviting us to do the hard work of communal remembering. This kind of labor demands a collective humility directly at odds with life in the flesh. Pride shrugs its shoulders in indifference, not wanting to be bothered by the racial pain of those who come from a legacy of suffering. Conversely, it is the humble person who wades into the pain.

ETHNIC UNITY DISCUSSION

Take a moment to think about the cultural scripts you've been handed, such as the socioeconomic status of the home you grew up in, your ethnicity, the schools you went to, etc., and share the following with the group:

How do your cultural scripts potentially hinder the work of ethnic unity?

How do your cultural scripts potentially help the work of ethnic unity?

Ask the group to speak into some potential blind spots, brought about by your cultural scripts, that you may have in the work of ethnic unity.

CHAPTER FOUR

THE PRACTICES OF ETHNIC UNITY

ONE OF MY FAVORITE BOOKS is by a South African pastor named Andrew Murray who lived in the nineteenth century. In his book *Humility*, he argues Jesus' core virtue is humility.[1] The incarnation itself demanded humility when Jesus left the comforts of heaven to take on flesh and live among us. Oh, the humility it took, when on the cross he submitted himself to abuse—even while legions of angels could have come to his rescue and thwarted his offenders. And yet he stayed. Paul mentions Jesus' humility to the Philippians when he says of our Savior, "And being found in human form, he humbled himself by becoming obedient to the point of death, even death on a cross" (Philippians 2:8).

Humility, Murray argues, is the proper estimation of oneself when compared to a holy God. Because humility is the antithesis of pride, and pride erodes relationships, humility enhances them. This is exactly Paul's point in Philippians 2:1-11. What must not be forgotten in what theologians call the "kenosis text," where Christ voluntarily veils aspects of his divine attributes (such as omnipresence), is the context. Paul is appealing to the church at Philippi to walk in unity. He calls them to walk in humility and then points to Christ and the incarnation as the penultimate example of what it means to be humble. To Paul, humility equals harmony.

ETHNIC UNITY REQUIRES HUMILITY

What does this look like in the context of ethnic unity? Let me offer several ways humility is needed. Humility, at times, serves not as a knife to harm but as a scalpel to heal. What this means is the humble person will engage in difficult conversations because their primary aim is not their acceptance, but the other person's growth. Humility, after all, is to be lowly, to live in subjection to someone or something else. For the Christian, being humble means bending our will not to the approval of others but to Christ and the gospel. So, when we see someone living in contradistinction to the life of Christ, humility compels us to say something.

One of the indicator lights of humility is the willingness to critique one's "own tribe." To be Black or Asian or White or Republican or Democrat is not to be infallible. No human political or ethnic group is beyond critique. We need people who are humble enough to call out the wrongs of their own ethnicity.

We see this in Acts 15 and the first church council. The issue they faced had to do with Gentiles coming to faith in Jesus who were being told by Jews they had to act Jewish (i.e., get circumcised and eat certain foods) in order to really be saved. The verdict from this church council—cast by a group of Jewish leaders—was a resounding, "No." Jews critiqued and corrected the error of fellow Jews.

We need White evangelicals to have the boldness to critique White evangelicalism when it errs. Where are the leaders who will speak prophetically to the heresy of Christian nationalism and remind many in their own tribe that Jesus does not stand and place his hand over his heart when America's national anthem is played? Where are the White evangelical leaders who, in christological humility, will declare Jesus is not returning on an elephant and that the kingdom of heaven does not nestle neatly inside the Republican Party?

We also need people of color who will walk in prophetic humility and challenge their ethnic kin to stop using their minority status as a set of handcuffs to hold our White siblings hostage to White guilt. I personally know of several minorities serving White churches who, if they were White, would have been fired a long time ago for legitimate reasons. But because they are people of color they get a pass, which results in stunted growth for themselves and the local church they are serving. Are there times to show vocational grace and patience? Of course, especially as the leadership, in seeking to understand and walk in unity among themselves, learns each other's unique cultural differences. But there comes a time when enough is enough. Perpetual victimhood serves no one well. What this necessitates are Spirit-filled minorities who will challenge the individual to repent of their flesh and surrender control to the Holy Spirit.

These things are not always popular. Being eager to maintain unity necessitates conflict. The work is constant, and time does not permit me to talk about the other ways in which we must apply the medicating balm of humility. It takes humility to forgive. Reconciliation likewise requires mutual humility. Extending grace to leaders who are learning through their public passivity or missteps also takes deep humility. I hope you are seeing the impossibility of ethnic unity without the soil of humility.

ETHNIC UNITY REQUIRES PATIENCE

The work of unity also requires patience. The Greek word Paul employs for patience is a compound that means "long toward anger." Scholars have pointed out the reason why we seldom pray for patience is that we understand such a request involves being placed in a situation we do not like—a situation that tests our anger. We don't learn patience during those rare seasons when the kids are being compliant. We don't learn patience when our significant other is treating us with respect and honor. And we don't learn patience when our job is going well and the bank account is full. Prosperity really is a poor teacher.

We keep living, though, and we find ourselves in circumstances where our anger is tested, especially in our relationships with others. The call to live in community is an invitation to do life with sinners—people who are guaranteed to fail us. And this becomes even more apparent when we try to walk in unity across the ethnic divide.

Patience has been described as the refusal to make someone move at your pace. The very notion of patience suggests a person whose anger is being tested because of their perception that the other person is not where they should be on a particular matter. More times than not, there are varying degrees of maturity involved. One *could* demand the other person speed up to where they are. But while this may work for relay runners on the track, one cannot simply speed up authentic maturity. We know this to be true because patience is an indicator light of the mature, Spirit-filled person.

When our children were just learning to walk, Korie and I were filled with excitement. We would stop everything, grab our camcorders (yes, this was in a pre-smartphone era), and remove anything that could cause our children to fall. We joyfully cheered them on, encouraging them to take another step. But at some point, of course, they fell. How did Korie and I respond? We didn't scream at our children and call them names. Nor did we just shake our heads, gather our camcorders, and leave the room while thinking, "You are just like your mother/father." Instead, we excitedly picked them up, consoled them, and encouraged them to try again. Our patience was a no-brainer because we assumed their immaturity.

Writing to the Colossians, Paul articulates his pastoral vision when he says he labors to "present everyone mature in Christ" (Colossians 1:28). Embedded in this vision is an essential implication: Paul assumes immaturity. Like parents with children who are stumbling through their inaugural steps only to inevitably fall, Paul sees himself as an encouraging pastor, cheering on newborn babes in Christ on their journeys into maturity. This is why the legendary pastor A. Louis Patterson observed the three pillars of all successful pastoral ministry are "patience with people, patience with people"—and you guessed it—"patience with people."

But patience is not reserved merely for leaders; it's for everyone. To the Galatians, Paul says patience is a necessary indicator light of the Spirit-controlled follower of Jesus. To the Ephesians, he couples patience with any assembly swimming to the shoreline of (ethnic) unity. Patience is laced with the assumption that the other person is not where they should be in regard to a certain issue.

Our generation has a zero-tolerance policy for anyone who is not "with it" concerning matters of racial justice and equality. People harbor no patience for the racially immature.

Now, please don't misunderstand me—people should be held accountable for their actions. Donald Sterling, former owner of the Los Angeles Clippers, should have lost his privilege as the owner of an NBA team because of the racist words he used and the environment he cultivated over the years. James, the brother of Jesus, warns in his epistle of the weightiness of words (James 3). Truly, there is power in the tongue.

Yet, as significant as our words may be, the tongue is not beyond the redeeming power of the gospel, nor is the heart, the fountainhead from which the tongue speaks. While someone may be (rightly) cast from their job, they should not be cast from the local family of God, the church, if they have a spirit of repentance. The Bible depicts sanctification as a process in which we are becoming more and more like Jesus. Our adventure into Christlikeness will be fraught with failure. We are alive at this moment, given not just a second chance (we used that up a long time ago), but another chance because of the inexhaustible patience of God.

The difference between Martin Luther King Jr.'s approach and the approach of others, such as the Nation of Islam or the Black Power movement, can be reduced to one word: *patience*. The work of "redeeming the soul of America" necessitated patience. People being bitten by dogs, people getting thrown in jail, children enduring thunderous streams of water in Birmingham, Alabama, and other unspeakable atrocities required a Spirit-induced patience, where Black Americans modeled deep maturity while exposing the petulance of White segregationists. For minorities, the possibility of home ownership or educational advancement at the school of our choosing rests on the patient shoulders of those who have gone before us.

As a reconciler, I know the fatigue of swimming to the shoreline of ethnic unity as I labor in predominately White evangelical spaces. For one particular entity I serve, I have been pushing for the previous decade plus, for a specific agenda that I believe will increase our efforts of ethnic unity significantly. Finally, we have experienced a breakthrough. The work has been wearisome but rewarding.

Once, I preached a sermon that caused a young White man from our church, Mike, to immediately email me expressing his deep concern that I had used the word *oppressor*. Now, the sermon had nothing to do with race, and my use of the term was describing Rome's relationship to the Jews. Mike was upset because he assumed I was taking a jab at White people. I responded by inviting him out to breakfast. A few days later, we found ourselves across from each other at a table in a local diner enjoying a meal. I began to probe him on his concern. When had I mentioned White people? Did race come up at all in the sermon, and if it did, what would be the problem since the Bible speaks to the issue? After some respectful back and forth, he concluded his anger had been spiked by the oppressed/oppressor binary, recently popularized by the critical race theory conversation. Therefore, Mike assumed my use of the word *oppressor* meant I was talking about race, an assumption he now realized was wrong. As we finished our meal, he thanked me with great humility for meeting with him and asked if we could connect again. I agreed.

If I can be honest with you, my flesh wanted to say, "I ain't got no time for this." As a Black man in these spaces, if I let my flesh call the shots, I would have never offered to meet with Mike and would have nursed yet another wound from someone I would have labeled as another insensitive person who doesn't get it. But all of this falls short of Paul's pastoral vision. This brother was immature in matters of race, having been more discipled by media and soundbites than by Jesus and the Scriptures. If we were going to have any hope of ethnic unity, I had to be patient.

Paul's context for life in the Spirit, of which patience is an attribute, is a relational one. Right on the heels of describing what the Spirit-filled life looks like, he says, "Brothers, if anyone is caught in any transgression, you who are spiritual should restore him" (Galatians 6:1). What's the specific transgression? We don't know, and I think therein lies the profundity of ambiguity. "Any transgression" encompasses racism. How would a spiritual person work to restore the racist who desires to be restored? "But the fruit of the Spirit is . . . patience" (Galatians 5:22). I hope you are seeing this kind of work ain't for the immature; it's for grown folks.

This raises an important question people often ask me: "How long do I have to hang in there?" Remember, the Bible calls us to patience, not passivity. There is a difference between not moving fast and not moving at all. When the culture of the church is at a standstill with no movement, they have become passive. Patience may require several church meetings, but if the church takes no action beyond mere words, God could very well be calling on you.

I would be remiss to not speak to my White brothers and sisters concerning the patience required of them toward people of color. When minorities speak out of their pain due to years of very real hurt and trauma, the majority of Whites are culturally conditioned to think, *That happened back then. It's a new day, so let's just get on with things*. When people muster up the courage to give voice to the racial trauma or discomfort they are feeling, White people need a Spirit-induced patience to cut against the grain of how they have been formed. It takes patience to genuinely listen and seek to not only sympathize but to even offer an apology. If you, my White sibling, want to know if you are filled with the Spirit, exhibiting the attribute of patience, how do you respond when a sermon given on race makes you uncomfortable? I cannot begin to tell you how many people I have seen leave one of my sermons on race, in a rush to send me a very terse note and scold me for my bad theology. I am not beyond rebuke, and there have been times when I failed to allow the fruits of love, kindness, and gentleness to envelop my words. But my failings aside, our White brothers and sisters are in need of patience as well.

Let us remember, the need for patience reveals the other person is not where they need to be on a particular matter. From a societal standpoint, the ugly history of America has given so many people good reason to be impatient. A cursory look at America's history should lead people to understand why minorities might hit the roof over an act of racism. When a person of color is part of a church or organization, they are more than likely coming with a set of experiences in which they have been hurt in regard to race, placing them in a unique position to their White counterparts. The conversation on patience is difficult because people of color have endured centuries of trauma, compared to their White siblings who have hardly, if any, racial hurt to work through.

I have seen White people exhibit God-glorifying patience toward minorities when the subject of race comes up. I have also witnessed grace-filled patience as White leaders go the extra mile vocationally with their minority staff because they are sincere in their journey into the beloved community. (As mentioned earlier, there is a time when enough is enough, and there is a time for patience and grace.) I have also witnessed my own fleshly impatience when I unleashed on my White brothers and sisters, in less than honorable ways, the racial hurt brimming in my own soul. While the pain of injustice is searing, the Spirit-controlled life does not give me, a Black man, a pass on how I express my pain. Truth, righteous anger, patience, humility, and gentleness (among others) can all coexist.

ETHNIC UNITY REQUIRES GENTLENESS

As we reach for the shoreline of ethnic unity, Paul exhorts Christ-followers to have gentleness. We often think of gentleness as the gift wrapping. But the Greeks understood gentleness to be more than the black velvet box encasing the diamond; they saw gentleness as also being the diamond. In other words, gentleness is not just the way a person comes across; it is also who the person is. This explains why Paul sees gentleness as an expression of the Spirit-filled life. The Holy Spirit is not just concerned with our exterior moral strivings; he is more so concerned with our interior life. Life in the Spirit is not white-knuckling patience or gentleness but rather *being* patient and gentle.

The Greek philosopher Aristotle argued the gentle person is not one who merely resists outward explosions of unrighteous anger. Nor is she the one who shrugs her shoulders in passive indifference. Instead, the Greek word for gentleness conveys a person who regulates their emotions in such a way that the humanity of the person they are in disagreement with is honored.[2]

The difference between a doctor and a murderer can be summed up in the word *gentle*. Both hold sharp objects that can take a person's life. One brings healing while the other brings death. Both objects are necessary to their work, but it all comes down to whether they are gentle—and their gentleness is informed by how they *view* the person at their mercy.

This is an important point. Life in the Spirit enhances relationships while life in the flesh erodes them. The Spirit-filled believer will always hold another person's humanity in high regard. In those "let's go there" moments when confrontation is a must, they will not diminish the humanity of the one they are in disagreement with, even the ethnic other. In other words, they will wield the scalpel of truth to bring ultimate healing even at the expense of momentary pain and discomfort.

But there is another extreme I must caution against. Sure, on one hand we must be careful against eruptions of unrighteous anger. But on the other hand, we must avoid passive indifference. I confess the latter is my struggle. When you have been engaged in the work of ethnic unity for as long as I have, and you've seen the underbelly of the Christian community where people often express an interest but don't do the hard work, it's easy to shrug your shoulders and assume the worst. Indifference does not honor a person's humanity either, because by very definition, to be indifferent is to give up on humanity.

Gentleness is essential to the work of reconciliation. It is the ability to express deep convictions in the face of opposition while showing honor to the other person who has been made in the image of God.

As a reconciler, I have found Dr. John Perkins to be a model of gentleness. Born in the Jim Crow South, Dr. Perkins saw the ugliness of racism firsthand. He was personally beaten by the White power structure, and while he convalesced, he had to decide whether he would wallow in bitterness or emerge in love. He chose the latter, and we are all the better for it. If you've ever heard him speak, he inevitably talks about race relations and the importance of reconciliation. The way he does so is full of conviction as he honors the timeless truth of God's Word and gentleness as he honors the humanity of the audience. Dr. Perkins has enjoyed a faithful ministry spanning decades as a vessel of reconciliation because of his Spirit-induced gentleness.

One reason we are not experiencing true ethnic unity in our churches, organizations, and society is that people fear being yelled at and mistreated if they express how they really feel. If the body of Christ was known for its gentleness, people would be more willing to share what they really think.

CONCLUSION

While laboring for ethnic unity, I've had to wrestle with this nagging question: Do I want to win more than I want unity? As with marriage, I've discovered oftentimes when *I* win, *we* lose. When another follower of Jesus says something racially insensitive, I have the choice to either blast them to prove how wrong they are and how right I am, or I can respond in such a way as to build a bridge, helping to realign their thinking with God's and setting the stage for unity.

I remember preaching at a very conservative church on the need to forgive. While the sermon was not on race explicitly,

I did share about a time a White brother wounded me deeply with his racism and how God led me to do the painful work of forgiving. Afterward, a White gentleman came up to me. Everything about his countenance conveyed he was disturbed as he exhaled, "Why is everything with you people about race?" How was I to respond? I could have made him feel small by wielding the scalpel of the Word of God to prove how wrong he was and how right I was. But I thought, *He doesn't get it, and maybe God wants me to help him.*

I gently asked him if he had any true friends who were people of color. He paused and confessed he didn't. I reminded him of the importance of ethnically different friendships because they create empathy, a trait he could use more of. His whole demeanor changed, and he agreed I had given him something to think about before he left.

I have no idea if he went on to build friendships with people of color. What I do know is after he left, I shook hands with several other White brothers of mine who had noticed the exchange and thanked me for how I handled him. They then proceeded to share very vulnerable things with me, many on the sensitive subject of race. It was clear they felt safe with me.

This is what happens when we lead with the trifecta of humility, patience, and gentleness. When winning is replaced with unity, when "I" becomes secondary to "we," we create space for the Spirit to do its work of humility, patience, and gentleness, and we reach the shoreline of ethnic unity.

ETHNIC UNITY DISCUSSION

Ethnic unity requires humility, patience, and gentleness. In a small group, begin by praying for each other that the Holy

Spirit will enable you to talk and listen with humility, patience, and gentleness. When you have disagreements, it's always helpful to pose questions instead of making statements.

Here are a few topics for discussion:

During the Covid-19 pandemic, there was rhetoric that referred to the virus as the "Chinese Virus." Does the church have a responsibility to speak against such language?

Do you find anything about the Black Lives Matter organization helpful? Harmful?

Should the sentiment (not the organization) "Black lives matter" be controversial?

Is racial injustice merely a matter of personal offenses, or is it also systemic? If you believe there are current examples of systemic injustice, share a few with the group and invite dialogue.

Note: These questions are provocative, to say the least. Before you engage with them, take a moment to pray and review the points on humility, patience, and gentleness, seeking to have these attributes, and ask the Holy Spirit to guide your conversation.

CHAPTER FIVE

BEWARE OF A NEW VISION WITH AN OLD CULTURE

IF YOU HAVEN'T PICKED UP on it by now, I *love* jazz. Our second son's name is Myles after Miles Davis. I wanted to name our youngest "Coltrane" after John Coltrane, but my wife told me I was doing too much and I needed to pump the brakes. You can't truly love jazz without knowing about one of the most important albums in jazz history: Coleman Hawkins's *Body and Soul*. Released in 1939, this album changed the culture of the medium. Prior to Hawkins's album, jazz in the big band era was dominated by structure and was somewhat methodical, even predictable. What made *Body and Soul* so unique is that Hawkins had the audacity to stray from the musical structure and venture out into improvisations that were foreign to many. In a word, Coleman Hawkins made jazz free.

Body and Soul is not just a great album, it is a culture-shifting album, leading many jazz historians to say a new era called bebop was ushered in. Bebop is the penultimate free expression in jazz, with little structure or rules, accompanied by fast tempos, advanced harmonies, and complex syncopations.

Musicians like Dizzy Gillespie and Charlie Parker sped through the green light of freedom Coleman Hawkins established, taking jazz to even greater extremes. The response to all of this was mixed. Younger people loved the new genre of bebop, flocking to clubs and venues to hear more. They could not get enough. The older "jazz purists" hated it, claiming bebop was an inferior product and would never last (oh, how wrong they were). When bebop was in its infancy, it was common to see older jazz lovers and musicians get up and walk out of the clubs never to return. Sadly, they were too locked into the older way of doing things to appreciate the new way.

This sort of reaction is hardly limited to jazz. When a new vision meets an inflexible culture, resistance is guaranteed. It's true in jazz, in business, and if you've been around church long enough, it's also true there.

Some years ago, a friend of mine became the pastor of a historic church in a prominent American city. Not long into his tenure, he shared with me his challenges of transitioning the culture of the church. His predecessor had been run out because their church is near a sports arena. The owner of the sports team that plays at the venue wanted to buy their church and demolish it to provide additional parking for the arena. The owner went on to offer well over market value for the church and proposed building them a new church only a few blocks away for the grand total of a dollar. Because their building was paid for, they would have pocketed several tens of millions of dollars.

Sounds like a great deal, doesn't it? Well, when my friend's predecessor took it to the congregation for the by-law required vote, it was voted down . . . almost unanimously. The reason? As a handful of the longtime members said, "My grandparents gave of their savings to help build this church. No way we are moving." Discouraged, the previous pastor tendered his resignation and moved on. Hearing this story from my friend who had just become the pastor and had so many plans he was eager to implement, I thought to myself, *Good luck*. A new vision with an inflexible culture is an equation for disaster.

This is important to remember as we wrestle with what it means to be an offensive church that storms the gates of hell, especially when it comes to race and ethnic unity. To simply cast the vision for ethnic unity at a church or organization, without doing the work to change the culture, is as useless as offering a historic church tens of millions of dollars to demolish its current edifice and build a new church without first addressing their hearts and culture. Preaching on ethnic unity a few times a year won't move the needle. It may even move the pastor out of the church if the culture hasn't been prepared.

But what is culture? Culture is a bit hard to define because it is the proverbial house we live in. Culture is a mixture of many elements like socioeconomic status, ethnicity, language, habits, and more. Culture is only really seen by those inside of it, while those outside of the culture question and challenge their way of doing things. When this happens, many will answer by digging in and saying, "This is the way we have always done it." When two opposing cultures meet up—when bebop blows its horn in a big band culture—we can expect a mess.

This idea of the messiness of a new vision meeting an inflexible culture is clearly laid out in Matthew 9:14-17, where

Jesus uses the analogy of new wine being poured into old wineskins. To appreciate the gravity of Jesus' words, we have to remember who he is talking to and why he came. Matthew writes his Gospel to religious Jews. The inference is important: never confuse the gospel with religion.

They are two completely different operating systems. The Jews were very religious people who went to the synagogue every week, worshiped at the temple on high and holy days, constantly offered sacrifices, memorized the first five books of the Bible, and gave close to 20 percent of their annual income to the things of God. They were some of the most moral people to have ever walked the face of the earth, and in spite of all this, Jesus came offering something even more culture shifting than Coleman Hawkins's *Body and Soul*. He offered them the gospel, their only hope for salvation. The gospel is not just a set of propositional truths but represents a whole new paradigm for seeing and navigating life. And how did these religious people respond? The same way the jazz purists did when they heard this new thing called bebop: they resisted.

We must keep this in mind when we read Jesus' words in Matthew 9:14-17:

> Then the disciples of John came to him, saying, "Why do we and the Pharisees fast, but your disciples do not fast?" And Jesus said to them, "Can the wedding guests mourn as long as the bridegroom is with them? The days will come when the bridegroom is taken away from them, and then they will fast. No one puts a piece of unshrunk cloth on an old garment, for the patch tears away from the garment, and a worse tear is made. Neither is new

wine put into old wineskins. If it is, the skins burst and the wine is spilled and the skins are destroyed. But new wine is put into fresh wineskins, and so both are preserved."

It's important to keep in mind the larger context of Matthew as we try to make sense of Jesus' analogy. Jesus is introducing something new: the kingdom of heaven, with the gospel as its operating system. The problem is this new vision is being met with resistance by the religious who are clinging to the old way. So, Jesus gives two analogies that capture exactly what he and the disciples are experiencing. In the first, he says no one should put a piece of unshrunk cloth on an old garment. The reason for this is obvious—as the unshrunk cloth begins to shrink, it will tear the old garment, which has already shrunk as much as it can. Then he says no one should put new wine into old wineskins. During the fermentation process, the wine emits gasses that put pressure on the wineskins. If the wineskins are new, they can stretch with the new wine. But if they are old and no longer have elasticity, they will explode and create a colossal mess. The common denominator in both analogies is the dire warning of paring old with new.

I must be clear that Jesus is not guilty of ageism. He is not saying people can't be used once they get to a certain age. Let's remember, Moses is about eighty years old when God gives him a fresh vision and a new assignment to lead Israel out of bondage and into freedom. Abraham is more than eligible for Medicaid when God calls him to be the father of the nation of Israel. And then there's my favorite, Caleb, who— when the nation of Israel is entering into the Promised Land and is divvying out lots—not only asks for the hill country but also wants to go to war and drive out the nations occupying the allotment of his inheritance. Many of our heroes in the faith were what we would today call elderly, and yet they embraced new-wine vision for their lives.

In Jesus' analogy of old wineskins, therefore, he is not speaking to the accumulation of birthdays in a person's life as much as he is to a lack of intellectual and emotional elasticity. Old-wineskin thinking locks in on the way things have always been done and refuses to entertain change. Old-wineskin thinking remains in the big band era and walks out when bebop is played. Sure, there are some things we must be "big band" about—the deity of Christ, the fact that he died in our place for our sins, and how salvation is by grace through faith. We don't need new wineskins for these essentials of the faith. However, *how* these things are communicated, including the methods we use and how we approach church, *must* have some elasticity. In my years of pastoral ministry, I have encountered both elderly people with new-wineskin mindsets and young people with old-wineskin thinking.

I'll never forget a particular family from our church that wanted to schedule a meeting with me. This family had three generations, had all moved down from the Midwest, and wanted to talk about my plans for the church being multiethnic. During our time together, I met the patriarch and matriarch of the family—a couple in their nineties who had been married for seventy years. As African Americans they had lived through the nightmare of Jim Crow. Now they felt compelled to come to our then–majority White church, roll up their sleeves, and help us become multiethnic—while in their *nineties*! Talk about "give me the hill country," new-wineskin kind of thinking.

I've also seen this work the other way. One of my colleagues had planted a thriving church and watched as it grew to thousands of mostly young people. His church happened to be in the South and was all White. Then God began to give him a new-wine vision for being multiethnic. Assuming the people would be with this new vision, he started hiring minorities on staff, changing some of the music, and preaching courageous sermons. He quickly lost around 30 percent of his young congregation. Finally, things reached a boiling point, and he was put out of his church. Clearing through the debris, one is left to conclude he had a young church with an old-wineskin mentality.

The principle Jesus gives is so helpful as we talk about the church being on the offensive in matters of ethnic unity. Jesus wants us to know a new-wineskin vision poured into an old-wineskin culture will create a huge mess. We must spend exponentially more time addressing the culture than word-smithing the vision.

HISTORICAL

The culture of every church has been formed deeply. The question is, Has the church been shaped in the way of Jesus or the way of the world? No follower of Christ enters into the church as a blank piece of paper. We bring all of our experiences and lack of experiences with us. Let me discuss three ways through which we have been shaped: history, media, and relationships.

Richard Wright was an African American writer who gifted us with classics such as *Native Son* and his autobiography, *Black Boy*. Born in the South, Wright experienced tragedy early on. His father abandoned his family for another woman, thrusting his mother into the workforce. Because she didn't make enough money, Wright teetered on the precipice of starvation for much of his childhood. What's more is that he was never really loved by his family, and especially not by Whites in the Jim Crow South. This created in him a deep hatred of Whites, which necessitated his enculturation in learning how to relate to Whites if he was going to survive. In a painful passage in his autobiography, Wright tells of the time his colleague approached him out of concern for how he was relating to Whites. If he did not change and adapt to the culture of the Jim Crow South, his friend reasoned, he would soon be hanging from a tree. He had to stop looking Whites in the eye. Wright needed to learn to address Whites by "sir" or "ma'am." And when walking down the sidewalk, if a White person was coming toward him, he needed to move out of the way. Reluctantly, Wright agreed.

Sometime later, Wright made his way to the North. When he arrived in Chicago, he was shocked to discover the culture was different. He was now in an environment where he could relate to Whites in much more egalitarian ways. He could look them in the eye and did not always have to address them by honorific titles like "sir" and "ma'am." Yet while he was free from the culture of the South, he found himself navigating Whites as if he were still there: "I was persisting in reading my present environment in the light of my old one."[1]

This is helpful for us as we discuss the very important matter of culture. When a person becomes a follower of Jesus, they instantly become a part of the new culture of the church, yet their way of viewing and navigating people of different ethnicities does not necessarily change immediately. More often than not, they will find themselves like Wright—thrust into the new culture of the people of God but relating to it as if they were in the old culture of the world.

If you are a White leader of an entity that is looking to become multiethnic, you need to know, broadly speaking, some minority groups will be hesitant to tell you all they are thinking and feeling toward you and other Whites. The reasons for this are multifaceted. For many minorities, like Asians, this could be due to the high value of honor their culture places on those in authority. But their reticence could also be born out of a lack of trust. Like slaves in the Antebellum South, or the help during the Jim Crow era, African Americans have grown adept at smiling and pretending everything is all right, while behind closed doors and in the exclusive company of their own, they unveil how they really feel.

I cannot tell you how many times I have seen this play out among churches aspiring to be multiethnic. I once worked with a church that had lost many minority staff for various reasons. The church leaders, feeling as if they were losing ground on their vision for ethnic unity, seemed hopeless. I called a closed-door meeting with all the people of color on staff. One of them said they didn't know how much longer they could hang in there. When I shared this with the White leaders of the church, they responded with disbelief. After all, none of the minority staff had disclosed this to them. I told them not to take it personally. Like Wright in the new environment of the North, people of color may often feel as if they are still in the old environment. It might not be right, but sadly it's true. It's a part of the culture.

This means the world when we talk about the new-wine vision of ethnic unity in an old-wineskin culture. While there

may be excitement when the church or organization an-
nounces its aim toward ethnic diversity and unity, it's ex-
pected that people of color will be somewhat hesitant. Again,
I'm painting with a broad brush, but the tradition of distrust
toward our White brothers and sisters is persistent. Plus, for
far too many minorities, we remember times when we let our
guard down only to be hurt by people who didn't come
through on their promises.

This is true not only for how people of color relate to Whites
in power but also interpersonally. Our White brothers and
sisters who we sit next to in church need to know they tend
to begin in the red with many minorities as well, especially
African Americans. This is a point Wright draws out from his
own experience:

> Misreading the reactions of whites around me made me
> say and do the wrong things. In my dealing with whites,
> I was conscious of the entirety of my relations with
> them, and they were conscious only of what was hap-
> pening in a given moment. I had to keep remembering
> what others took for granted; I had to think out what
> others felt.[2]

Wright was on pins and needles around Whites, always
viewing their actions through the lens of their ethnicity and
thereby having to play chess as a Black man in order to culturally survive. This, he says, was not a two-way street. Whites
were not on edge in their relations with them. Again, not
right, but true.

For example, look no further than the premium Blacks
place on being greeted and spoken to, particularly in majority White church settings. Granted, no one likes to be

ignored. And yet, I cannot tell you the disproportionate number of times Blacks have been disappointed and even left a predominately White church because they felt they were not spoken to, compared to our White siblings. Why is this? If we are really honest, we feel as if we are working at a deficit with them—we perceive that White people think they are better than us. As a result, when one of our White brothers or sisters in church does not speak to us, we automatically assume they feel superior to us, all while they have no clue what is happening. I am not saying most Whites in the church feel they are better than people of color. Rather, I am saying for many Blacks it is a projected perception that has become reality.

Doing the math? Whites are starting at a deficit with Blacks. Because many Blacks subconsciously assume Whites think they are better than them, Blacks then assume they are working from a deficit with Whites. And if you are Asian or Latino or any other minority, you feel pressure to choose a side on the Black/White binary. In this old-wineskin culture, leaders want to get up and announce the new-wineskin vision of ethnic unity, totally oblivious to the powerful cultural undercurrents at work in their congregation. As my grandmother liked to say, "Bless their heart."

MEDIA

Of course, there are other factors that make it hard for people to embrace the new-wineskin vision of ethnic unity. While each of us has been historically formed by race, we are also dealing with social media platforms such as Twitter and TikTok, the media, and politics, which often run counter to the new-wineskin vision Jesus wants us to embrace.

In a *New York Times* opinion piece, David Brooks speaks to the influence media has on followers of Jesus:

> Over the past couple of decades evangelical pastors have found that their 20-minute Sunday sermons could not outshine the hours and hours of Fox News their parishioners were mainlining every week. It wasn't only that the klieg light of Fox was so bright, but also that the flickering candle of Christian formation was so dim.[3]

Obviously, we would do well to lengthen his example of Fox News to include social media and other media outlets like MSNBC and CNN, to name a few, but his point still stands: we cannot be surprised when Christians dig in and do not embrace the new-wine vision of ethnic unity, not when they are being formed as tribes that are often established along political and racial lines. The decision to spend more time at the feet of people like Don Lemon, Laura Ingraham, and Chris Matthews has given birth to a church that is more fluent and passionate about the politics of this world than the kingdom of heaven. The result is not unity but division.

What happens to a person who is being discipled more by the media than the Messiah? They begin to view the world through their discipler, even using their language. I've never been accused of critical race theory or been called a cultural Marxist by political progressives, but I have by conservatives. And I've never heard someone who ingests large, daily, exclusive doses of Fox News or Newsmax gratuitously use phrases like *white supremacy* and *white privilege*. To be sure, media has its place, but when we don't filter media through the Bible, we will filter our Bible through our media. And we can, therefore, assume division, because we have been formed away from Jesus and into the world.

RELATIONSHIPS

In addition to history and the media, our relationships shape us. These relationships take on a historical component, especially in terms of our families of origin. Pete Scazzero, a former pastor, has done wonderful work looking at how our emotional health intersects with spirituality and the ongoing influence our homes wield over us—influence that does not stop the moment we leave home.[4] It really is true: Jesus may live in our hearts, but Grandpa resides in our bones.

It was in this context that I first learned powerful lessons about how I relate to the ethnic other. I grew up in a home where my parents never said anything bad about White people or any person of any other race. They also modeled multiethnic relationships and what it looks like to care about people who look and view life differently than you. But all this aside, I had to learn some very painful lessons on race on my own.

I grew up in a small Southern town on the outskirts of Atlanta. When I was in ninth grade, I liked a White girl. When my father found out, he gave me some stern words of caution, warning me that not everyone saw the world as he and my mother did and I would want to think more circumspectly of this relationship. I was shocked. Looking back, I shouldn't have been. I grew up in the South in the late 1980s, just a few decades removed from the civil rights movement.

But hey, who listens to their father at fourteen? I continued the relationship—if indeed you can call it that when all we did was get dropped off at the mall to window shop and eat at the food court. Sure enough, her father found out about me, phoned, and called me a "Black son of a . . ." I immediately went to my father expecting him to get in the car, drive to his home, and give him a good evangelical cussing out. Instead, I was met with his version of "I told you so." The message I learned that day I carried with me for years: Whites will never fully accept you.

Jesus may live in my heart, but I carry my father and lessons like these in my bones. So do you. Granted, you may have grown up in a very inclusive home that valued people of all ethnicities. This is becoming more and more true the younger a person is. But the short sermon I received from my dad on race is something many people of color get—a message of extreme caution when it comes to Whites.

Many Asians are taught to simply be quiet, blend in, and be successful, never expressing how they really feel in the process. This is an assimilation strategy in which they learn to keep their heads down lest they call attention to themselves and get attacked. Many Whites are given a cultural script of fear when it comes to people of color, which works against experiencing authentic relationships with the ethnic other. Not long after my girlfriend's father called me a son of a female dog, he made his daughter cut off all her hair and moved her some five hours away to live with her mother. I was heartbroken. Years later, I would realize the narrative of fear that runs so pervasively among our White siblings' perceptions of people of color. This and more work against us coming together in ethnic diversity and unity to embrace the new-wine vision of the gospel.

While the multiethnic church has been growing, it is still a minority in the ecclesiological landscape. The homogeneous church is still king in America by a long shot. Our Sunday morning homogeneity reflects our relational homogeneity.

Scholars have observed that one of the dangers of the homogeneous church is its propensity to entrench our biases and presuppositions. We all have them when it comes to just about everything. And to be in an environment where, broadly speaking, everyone holds the same views on politics, economics, and race is not good for our personal growth and development. In other words, we need people in our lives who see things differently as a means to our own formation.

Distance breeds suspicion. When we do not live in community with those who are different, we will by nature otherize them. And when someone is otherized, the table is set for fear, racism, classism, and so on.

This is not the way of Jesus. When he came to bring the new-wine vision of the gospel, he did so in an environment of a fixed social order reflected most intensely during mealtimes. Who you ate with was a statement of status. Because of this, you would never catch the rich eating with the poor, or the ceremonially clean with the ceremonially unclean. The tribal lines were fixed.

Jesus unsettled all of this. Have you noticed his most combative moments took place in a setting that was supposed to be one of peace and joy—the dinner table? The religious elite critiqued him for eating with tax collectors and sinners. They questioned his credentials as a rabbi when he allowed a prostitute at a party to clean his feet. And his own disciples were baffled their Lord would take on the form of a servant and clean *their* feet. Jesus' actions were intentional in each of these instances. He was sending the new wine, culture-shifting message of inclusiveness. Like Coleman Hawkins,

Jesus picks up his horn and casts a countercultural vision, boldly proclaiming that in the body of Christ there is no room for otherizing. Rich and poor, clean and unclean—we all come to the table, with Jesus as our head.

In a sense, then, the table of God is diverse. But remember, diversity for the sake of diversity will not last. It won't form us into the way of Jesus. Rather, our commitment to stay at the table and enmesh ourselves into one another's narratives is when rich spiritual formation happens.

Such a commitment has a way of de-forming us away from the world and forming us into the way of Jesus. This is why Paul planted multiethnic churches, like the one at Philippi, where the first converts were a wealthy woman named Lydia, a slave girl, and a Philippian jailer. The church at Philippi is just one of many in what became a normative pattern of Paul planting multiethnic churches. Sure, he could have started several churches in the same city and catered to the felt ethnic needs of Jews and Gentiles. If Paul was motivated to create a megachurch, he would have conformed the gospel to the social norms and sensibilities of his day. No doubt the results would have been very twentieth-century American—large! But Paul made a decision every leader must wrestle with when it comes to the new-wineskin vision of being multiethnic: Do you want to be mega or multiethnic? Very rarely does this choice become a both/and; in just about every instance, it is an either/or.

To Paul and the leaders of the first church, the local assembly was not a place to merely sing songs and receive great sermonic content; it was a community with rich relationships. So substantive were their interactions that a term was coined to describe what they were experiencing: *koinonia*, or what we would today translate as fellowship. At its core, *koinonia* is held together by a sense of mutuality or commonness, which transcends difference. *Koinonia* is maintained by the magnetism of Christ, which serves as an irresistible gravitational force compelling people from diverse backgrounds toward each other.

In chemistry speak, *koinonia* contains an emulsifier. Mayonnaise is made up of things that don't mix, like oil and water. So how does one get oil and water to hang out together in close community? The answer is the emulsifier of egg. Emulsifiers bring things of different properties together in close community. The egg says, "Come here, oil, and hang out with me. Come here, water, and home in on me." The next thing we know, these disparate entities are experiencing *koinonia* with one another because of the emulsifier of egg.

Our Christian conviction is that Jesus is our emulsifier. His love for all humanity, his sacrifice and death on the cross, his resurrection on the third day and his ascension into heaven, his intercession on our behalf, and the promise of his return serve as the epicenter and emulsifier for Christian community. What brings us together is not the wonderfully wordsmithed new-wine vision of ethnic unity, but Jesus. In fact, any appeal to unity is not a plea to do something new but to walk in something declared centuries ago, when our Lord and Savior prayed in John 17 for our oneness.

In short, the emulsifier of Jesus transcends any cultural narratives we have been handed, particularly as it informs our perceptions and relations with the ethnic other. For those who were raised with a very real fear of a certain ethnic group, you must know the centrality of love and that *agapē* love casts out fear. For those who have been taught to assume others are better than you, you must come to terms with how God so loves you that he sent his only son to die for you. Marinating in John 3:16 is one of the best things anyone could ever do to combat the voices of inferiority. For those who feel marginalized, read through the Bible and you will discover there are well over two thousand verses that talk about God's heart for the poor, the widow, the orphan, and the immigrant. And for those who have an air of superiority about them, you should steep in passages such as Acts 2:42-47, where the emulsifier of the gospel not only brings rich and poor together but also compels those with material resources to divest themselves in order to provide for those without. Tim Keller is right to observe that righteousness in the Bible is disadvantaging oneself for the advantage of others.

When we consider these matters, we are confronted with an embarrassing truth: old-wineskin culture that resists the new-wineskin vision of ethnic unity doesn't just have a racial problem but ultimately a gospel problem, where the primacy of Jesus Christ has been usurped by cultural preferences and norms. It is the multiethnic church, committed to a robust discipleship that is concerned with forming people vertically into the image of Christ while walking in ethnic unity horizontally as members of the body of Christ, that offers the deepest apologetic to the world concerning the veracity of the gospel. Or to articulate its antithesis: people will not hear the truth of our gospel if they are not witnessing the love of our gospel—a kind of love that transgresses ethnic and tribal lines.

NO ETHNIC HOME TEAM

I have to believe we want this. We want to be part of a church or organization that has ventured well past superficial tolerance and diversity and has done the hard work of ethnic unity. But the line of demarcation between *aspiring* toward ethnic unity and *experiencing* ethnic unity can be summed up in the word *courage*. It's one thing to cast the new-wine vision of leaving Egypt; it's another thing to take up arms and fight the many nations occupying the Promised Land. God knew this, which is why he tells Joshua to "be strong and courageous." Reading the Bible, it's overwhelming how many times the refrain to not fear—and its implicit command to be courageous—is given. The lesson is clear: no one can execute new-wine vision without courage. Anyone can cast a vision off excitement or the anger-induced adrenaline rush of some national tragedy like the death of George Floyd. But the day-to-day work of kneading a culture to receive this vision requires an immense amount of courage and focus. While I will address these matters later, for now I will lay out several things we must do.

It bears repeating that culture is the house we live in. Yet, herein lies the problem. Culture is the attempt to create a sense of home. People often choose a church because it feels like home. This is why the three most influential culture-forming forces in the church—leadership, music, and preaching—also determine whether someone will lock arms and commit to the local assembly of Christ-followers.

I tell church planters all the time that from the day you begin to work on your church plant, imagine wet concrete being poured. The concrete represents the culture of your church: the amalgamation of decisions you make and don't make. In three years, the concrete will dry, and you will be who you are. Period. The work you do in these inaugural years are some of the most critical in the life of your church. Making any substantive changes after this season is akin to shattering a sidewalk to bits with a jackhammer. While this may be necessary, it's also traumatic.

While the concrete was still being poured on this new thing called the church, the leaders noticed a disturbing trend that centered around the question of culture. Jewish leaders were infiltrating these churches and telling new Gentile converts they needed to act Jewish in order to be saved. They whispered in their spiritually infantile ears about adhering to the works of the law. They said they needed to get circumcised. These Jewish leaders wanted the new-wineskin message of the gospel to inhabit the old-wineskin culture of Judaism.

When word of this got back to the church leaders, a church council was called, discussions were had, and a verdict was rendered. The consensus was Gentiles did not need to act Jewish in order to be Christlike. In other words, there was to be no ethnic or cultural home team.

Please notice that Jews were the ones who banged the gavel and gave the decision. It would have been more than convenient for these Jewish men to acquiesce to the schemes of the Judaizers who were trying to make sure these churches were culturally Jewish. Peter, James, John, and Paul had grown up in the synagogue. And yet, they as Jews were the biggest advocates for emancipating the church from its culturally Jewish captivity.

This is a truth we must incarnate. It has to get in our bones. When a majority White church wants to make a major cultural change to achieve ethnic unity, the White leadership must lead the way. You can't outsource this work to a minority hire, placing all the burden on them without empowering them at the same time. I've seen too many examples where a church composed mostly of one ethnicity, in trying to become multiethnic, hires a person of another ethnicity and expects them to lead the way. It seldom works. Acts 15 tells us that to challenge the culture, those who most benefit from the current culture must lead the way. In other words, while we acknowledge an all-White-led church (or any mono-ethnically led entity seeking to be diverse) will not experience true ethnic diversity and unity, we cannot go to the other extreme and assume hiring a few minorities will accomplish the mission. The new minority hires must be endowed with the power and resources needed to push the church forward into its desired future.

A ROBUST GOSPEL

This now brings us to the crux of the matter. If we are going to change the culture of our church so it moves into the new-wine vision of ethnic unity, the local body must make commitments to three things: a robust gospel, reliable leadership, and relational environments. The mission, leadership, and community are irrefutable elements in the process of the cultural formation that go to war with the old-wineskin cultural forces at work within the local assembly.

What follows in these pages is a strategic unfolding of new-wineskin culture. A robust gospel encompasses both the vertical and horizontal elements of the gospel. In my doctoral dissertation, I was curious to know how people of color—especially minority communities, which entail the culturally marginalized—understand the gospel compared to those who are in the majority. My research revealed what I intuitively knew: our White siblings often see the gospel in strictly vertical dimensions, while those on the fringes see it as also inhabiting horizontal outcomes.

Being a follower of Jesus is ultimately not about our relationship with God. In other words, God did not send his Son to die on the cross for us to merely experience better quiet times and to enhance our lives. This is a completely American notion. The phrase "my personal relationship with God" does not appear in the Bible, nor is it palatable to Eastern communities such as the ones in which the Scriptures are situated. Peruse the modern literature on spiritual formation, and we will reach the un-American conclusion that we are formed into the image of Christ not to be better versions of ourselves but to better those around us. M. Robert Mulholland had it right when he defined spiritual formation as "a process of being formed in the image of Christ *for the sake of others*."[5]

It is important to understand the Bible is always about the vertical and the horizontal. We see this with the Ten Commandments, as the opening laws of the Decalogue are vertical while the latter half is horizontal. The inference is explicit: we cannot refrain from adultery, coveting, or stealing unless we are first in right relationship with God. In Psalm 15 when the psalmist writes of the kind of person who experiences the fullness of their communion with God, he is quick to say they should be in right relationship with God and then with their neighbor. Jesus' plea for his followers to leave their gift at the altar and first be reconciled to their brother links their right standing with God in worship (vertical) with their proper standing with their horizontal fellow image bearer. What's more, Peter instructs husbands to stop praying to God (vertical) if their horizontal relationship with their wives is not what it should be. Peter's message is astounding: we and God are not right if we and our spouse are not right. More can be said along these lines. The Bible knows nothing of a greedy Christian, an unforgiving Christian, or a racist Christian. The pairing of these adjectives with the word *Christian* is both deeply troubling and oxymoronic. How we relate to God and others matters. In fact, the only way we can really ascertain how we are doing with God is through the lens of our relational status with others.

Leaders of entities desiring to be multiethnic will often hear cries of, "Why are we talking about this? We should just preach the gospel." Wrong and amen. The gospel is not just about getting into heaven. If it were, then God would have saved us and carried us to our eternal abode all at once. Instead, he left us here on earth so that our vertical relationship with him might yield horizontally transformative results until he comes again.

What now follows is crucial to our understanding of the necessity of any diverse church that seeks ethnic unity. Justice must be viewed not as an optional extra but as an apologetic—a defense of the gospel. What I mean by this is that marginalized communities will hear nothing of the gospel unless it lovingly addresses the felt needs of their oppressed communities. The philosopher Cornel West is spot on when he says justice is what love looks like in public.[6]

I have a family member who is at an impasse when considering a relationship with God. The issue troubling them is what theologians call theodicy—how can a so-called good God allow bad things to happen to "good people"? I could tell my family member to get over themselves, but this would be spiritual malpractice. Instead, I must be ready to give a defense for the hope that lies within. I must provide answers to their questions.

In the same way, the poor and racially oppressed need answers for the chasm between what they deserve and what they are experiencing. To merely dismiss their questions with soliloquies on the evils of critical race theory is likewise spiritual malpractice and grossly at odds with the teachings of Scripture and the way of Jesus. Let us not forget the apex of the Nation of Islam coincided with the passivity of who Dr. Martin Luther King Jr. described in his prison epistle as the "white moderate," or today, the conservative evangelical. If we are concerned with people's souls, we must address questions pertaining to their bodies. A robust gospel deals with both.

Tom Skinner began his public ministry as an evangelist in Harlem, back in the 1960s. In his memoir *Black and Free*, he talks of packing historic venues such as the Apollo Theater in Harlem with Black bodies to tell them the good news of Jesus Christ. At the same time, he also spoke prophetically to the injustices done to their bodies. The result was a Christocentric vision of the kingdom, one which followed the lineage of Jesus, who addressed both the souls of people when he called them to repent and their bodies when he fed, healed, and clothed them.

Before we start casting the new-wine vision of ethnic unity, the soil of the congregation must be cultivated continuously with the teaching of the gospel, whose message of the kingdom is bigger than us as individuals. God did not save us so we could sit in our favorite recliner, sip our morning cup of coffee, and enjoy our favorite Bible study program. While that is an inaugural step, it hardly represents the end zone of spiritual formation.

RELIABLE LEADERSHIP

Any entity that aspires toward the new-wineskin vision of ethnic unity has been gifted with leadership that serves as the custodians of both the vision and the robust gospel. As

my father has said, to be a leader is to be the visual representation of the destination the followers aspire to arrive at. A
burdensome statement, but true nevertheless.

Nothing of eternal significance happens without Christlike
leadership. Being a leader means incarnating the very values
you seek to instill in those who are following you. It is impossible to take people to a destination I am not traveling toward
myself. What made Paul so successful as a multiethnic church
planter is that he cultivated a multiethnic life, enjoying rich
koinonia with people he once regarded to be ceremoniously
unclean. And where did Paul's vision of the multiethnic, multicultural family of God come from? His leader, Jesus, who sat
at a well with a Samaritan woman, invited himself over to the
home of a rich and unscrupulous tax collector, and finally
died for the sins of the world.

The vision and values of any church or organization cannot
merely be outsourced to another staff person. They must be
incarnated by all of the leaders, especially the senior leader.
The many churches and organizations I've worked with over
the years that nurture grand visions of ethnic unity make the
same mistake over and over when they request my help with
hiring minorities to lead the charge in being multiethnic. I
understand and can sympathize with their sentiments. Implicit in their requests is the acknowledgment that they have
not been prepared by their family of origin and current life
experiences to lead the way into ethnic unity. Yet, when Paul
walked into places like Athens, Corinth, and Ephesus to plant
what would become flourishing multiethnic churches, he was
not drawing on a lifetime of rich inclusive experiences. Paul,
formerly known as Saul, grew up as both an ethnic and religious Jew. He had been taught to avoid Gentiles, especially

the non-God-fearing types. It would be no stretch to say he grew up racist and continued to harbor a very demeaning disposition toward the uncircumcised, up until his Damascus Road collision with Christ. And yet, almost immediately, he cultivated cross-ethnic friendships, planted multiethnic churches, and called out the cowardice and racism of fellow leaders who shirked their responsibilities as fellow shareholders in the new-wineskin vision of the multiethnic kingdom of God.

Paul did not hire someone safe he could hide behind to reach all people with the gospel and shepherd them into the new humanity of God. On one hand, Acts 6 is instructive and helpful on how to navigate multicultural conflict in the church when the ethnic other is appointed to address the problems. And while there is wisdom in that, on the other hand, overseeing it all was a group of Jewish leaders who were very much in process themselves, enmeshed in the narrative of the multiethnic community of faith.

If you are a majority leader of a majority church seeking to become multiethnic, always remember: while you will be wise to hire minority staff to match the desired demographic you are trying to reach, at the end of the day the congregation will examine how you live as permission for how *they* must live. Your commitment or lack thereof to the new-wineskin vision of ethnic unity will broadcast clearly whether this is simply something nice to do or something they have to do.

There is, therefore, a cost to leadership. What made the civil rights movement so effective was that its leaders were all in and willing to pay the price. They were beaten, jailed, and jeered at, and King ultimately died as a martyr because he inhabited the vision of equality. It has been said that during the last decade of King's life, any Black home would have a copy of the King James Bible and a picture of Dr. King. He was that beloved. When leaders sacrifice, it ingratiates them to their followers.

If one were to look a little closer, one would see all was not well within the movement the last years of King's life. People like Stokely Carmichael and others had grown weary of nonviolence and impatient in their quest for equality. Shouts of "Black Power" began to escalate, and King felt pressure from within to rethink his values and commitment. But he would have none of it. Unwavering to the end, King continued to incarnate his values of nonviolence and equality. His commitment put him at odds with many young emerging Black leaders of the Student Nonviolent Coordinating Committee and with President Johnson himself because of his stance against the war in Vietnam. King was not governed by what was popular but by what he deemed to be right. His reliable, courageous, incarnational leadership changed our nation.

Leaders must choose if they want to be measured by the "nickels and noses" of church giving and attendance or by a deep conviction of what is right. The pulpit is not the place to work out one's self-esteem issues. Just as some of the most effective evangelists are the newly converted, so can one be deeply effective when newly convinced within the depths of their soul of the new-wineskin vision of ethnic unity.

RELATIONAL ENVIRONMENTS

The gospel and leadership are essential elements in forming culture. So are relationships. We all have a longing to know and be known. At the same time, we all have a love/hate relationship with community. Traveling with what Pastor Gordon

MacDonald calls "our happy few" is both our source of deepest desires and most intense sorrows.[7] We feel this viscerally.

I know I do. If you were to ask me about my most transformative experiences, I would point you to my happy few. As a seminary student newly relocated to Southern California, I found myself spending two hours on Sunday afternoons at our church, seated in a circle with other men my age. We all were either grad students or young professionals, trying to make sense of life and live authentically for Jesus. We began each session sharing the struggles and failures we had encountered since our last gathering. We discovered the accuracy of C. S. Lewis's assessment of relationships when he said all friendships begin on a note of "you too."[8] We quickly formed a bond as we were drawn in by the universal struggles of humanity so freely shared during those Sundays in Inglewood.

Years later, the bond continues. We are on a group text thread where we check in weekly with each other, and once a year we fly in from across the country, now as middle-aged men, to laugh, cry, and encourage one another. I am who I am not just because of the Bible I read and preach, or the God I believe in and pray to, but also because of the people I let in to know me and the men who let me in to be known.

Part of the reason why community can be so cumbersome and sorrowful is that sin is not just personal but social. Adam and Eve hide from God and each other the moment they sin, meaning their vertical relationship with God and their horizontal relationship with each other are both impaired. The death of every marriage and the cause of every fractured relationship can be reduced to a three-letter word with "I" right in the middle of it: *sin*. This is important to remember when dealing with old-wineskin culture, which has proven to be hostile to the new-wineskin vision of ethnic unity. Racism is so insidious because it is a social barrier to the beloved community. Like it or not, we have all been deeply scarred by the pervasive culture of racism in America, no matter how "with it" we may think we are. Because of this, there is no way to ready the culture to receive the new-wineskin vision of ethnic unity without addressing the issue of relationships. No amount of reading about race, visiting museums on the history of racism, or hearing messages preached on race can substitute for the power of multiethnic relationships. This kind of eclectic community is the secret sauce to ethnic unity.

My father was once in a car accident in which the other driver was clearly at fault. Disoriented from the airbag, Dad emerged from his vehicle only to be met with a barrage of racial epithets from the older White man who had hit him. Still seething with anger some hours later, my father found himself at lunch across the table from one of his closest friends. In deep anguish, Dad exhaled, "Why is it at the end of the day to so many people, I will always just be a n_____?" Dad's friend listened and consoled. Soon, Dad's anger receded and was replaced by an otherworldly love toward his offender—a kind of love that led him to forgive him and share the gospel in court with this man. Dad's healing began with having lunch with one of his closest friends who happened to be White.

We hurt in isolation but heal in community. Sometimes relationships change our convictions or perspectives, but many times they do not. What relationships ultimately do is change how we relate to those on the other side of the aisle. While my convictions haven't changed regarding our friends in the gay community, how I preach and engage them most certainly has.

The catalyst for the change was a friendship my wife and I formed with a lesbian couple who became like family to us. The same holds true for the political, ethnic, and all kinds of "others" who have now become family because of the gospel.

What must not be lost on us, however, is that both the source and the antidote to my father's pain was found in cross-ethnic encounters with his White siblings. Like vaccines, the cure to our relational maladies is found in its very discomfort and pain. We have no other recourse but to lean into what we are repelled by. Multiethnic relationships are the path toward our de-formation away from how America has crafted us and our reformation in the way of Jesus toward the ethnic other. The church and its commitment to soul-level *koinonia* offer the only true hope for the world.

While we can podcast sermons, we cannot podcast community. There is something about being physically together that cannot be replaced by technology in how we grow as people. Some may push back and say they do not need to go to church to have a genuine relationship with Jesus. But we must remember the church is often referred to analogously as the bride of Christ. As one who has spent many days away from home traveling for work, it has never crossed my mind to say to my bride, Korie, "I do not need to come home to be married." No amount of time talking on the phone can replace sitting next to her on the sofa. Proximity— geographical closeness—is paramount to our oneness. The same rings true for the local body of Christ.

We must keep this in mind when we revisit letters like 1 and 2 Corinthians, Galatians, and Ephesians. Paul's words in these specific letters are addressed to bodies of people situated in close physical proximity to one another. They are not letters written to individuals (though some like Philemon, Timothy, and Titus are, and while they were addressed to individuals, they were also circulated to a wider audience). What's more, these letters are written not just to a community but to an eclectic, multiethnic one made up of Jew and Gentile. Paul calls them to push away from how they were culturally and ethnically formed across the divide and draw near to one another by the magnet of the gospel now inhabiting their lives.

CONCLUSION

In his classic *Mere Christianity*, C. S. Lewis follows the new-wineskin analogy of the culture-shifting vision Jesus gives of the gospel: "God became man to turn creatures into sons: not simply to produce better men of the old kind but to produce a new kind of man. It is not like teaching a horse to jump better and better but like turning a horse into a winged creature."[9] At its core, the gospel stands in contradistinction to every other world religion or human philosophy. The gospel, therefore, provides an unprecedented framework for all of life, especially in how we relate to each other. The first church got this, which is why former enemies sold what they had to give to those who did not have. What Luke documents at the end of Acts 2 was so astonishing it served as the catalyst to the church's explosive growth. People had never seen rich and poor, Jew and Gentile relate to one another like this in their tribal culture. The people of God were not solely being formed vertically in their relationship with him but also horizontally in how they viewed and approached life with one another. They were being formed into a new humanity.

In our cultural moment when so many are divesting themselves of the church, in what some have called "deconstruction,"

I can't help but think that if we allowed our gospel culture to rise to the level of our gospel doctrine, such deconstructing would not be needed. When we as followers of the Way allow the gospel to do its work of reforming us, and leaders do the persistent work of cultivating, we will create churches receptive to the new-wineskin vision of ethnic unity.

ETHNIC UNITY DISCUSSION

When you think of your church, would you say there is an "ethnic home team"—a group of people that the leadership, preaching, and style of music naturally cater to? Conservatives or liberals? Affluent or poor? One particular ethnicity?

Does the community in which your church is located match the demographics of the church?

What are some specific things your church could do to ensure there is no "ethnic home team"?

We have all been shaped in many ways when it comes to how we view and navigate race. One of the most powerful forces is our family of origin. How has your family of origin formed you in how you view and navigate race? Were you raised to be colorblind? Suspicious? Fearful? Healthy? Share a few examples.

CHAPTER SIX

PROCLAIMING A ROBUST GOSPEL

ETHEL WATERS WAS ONE OF THE GREATEST blues singers, not just because she had otherworldly talent but because she also lived the blues. Born in 1896, Ethel grew up in the church, where at the age of twelve she walked the aisle and submitted her life to Christ. Later that same year, she was forced by the people in her church into an arranged marriage. At the tender age of thirteen she left the church, vowing never to return.

What Ethel lived through can only be described as spiritual and physical abuse. Ultimately, she would channel her trauma into singing and acting, becoming the first African American woman to receive equal billing on Broadway and the second to be nominated for an Academy Award. And yet, she could not ignore the eerie sensation something was missing in spite of all her money, success, and accolades.

In 1957, Ethel was in New York when a tall, lanky preacher named Billy Graham was in town for what would become one of his most successful crusades ever. It did not start as he had hoped, however. Hardly any Blacks were showing up. A Black pastor friend of his told him he was getting exactly what he was projecting: The music was led by Whites. The people on the platform and the counselors were all White. If Graham wanted Blacks to come, he was going to have to change the culture. So he did. He invited Dr. Martin Luther King Jr. to share with him on the platform and took his crusade to Harlem.

In the midst of all these changes, an aging Ethel Waters, now in her sixties, wandered in and broke her vow of never returning to church. What she heard she could not summarily dismiss. When the time came, she walked the aisle for the second time in her life and rededicated herself to Christ. For the final twenty years of her life, she could be found at Graham's crusades singing, giving her testimony, and exuding an otherworldly joy—a kind of joy she could never find on a Broadway stage or behind a microphone, but only in the gospel of Jesus Christ.

What kept Ethel Waters out of church was the same thing that drew her back to church: Christian culture. We don't know what her childhood church preached in regard to the gospel. We do know what they practiced was in conflict with the gospel. And we know the universal gospel Graham preached was only yielding ethnically homogeneous fruit in the early days of his New York City campaign. So he had to do some hard work to align the culture with his doctrine, and when he did, Ethel came back to the place she had once left.

Gospel culture trumps gospel doctrine all day long. Regardless of what the doctrinal statement says on your website, or whether your church is Reformed or Wesleyan, people will choose to leave or stay based on how others in the church treat one another. Of course, I'm not saying doctrine doesn't matter. Yes, we should codify the essentials of the faith. And sure, the people need to be instructed in the whole counsel of God, which entails a right understanding of Jesus, salvation, and the nature of God. All I'm saying is, people may read your doctrinal statement and listen to a few messages on your website before they visit, but whether they stay depends on how those statements and messages are put into practice by the people they sit beside. Culture crushes doctrine all day long.

Some years ago, I was driving to church to preach for a friend of mine when I got distracted and began to drift into the adjoining lane. Evidently, I almost hit another car because the person inside honked his horn, pulled up alongside me, spoke to me very clearly in "sign language," then sped ahead. At the next light he turned right, and so did I. A few blocks later he hung a left, and so did I. *Oh no*, I thought. Sure enough, we both pulled into the church parking lot. I took it upon myself to park near him and wave, and he acted as if he didn't see me. An hour or so later I stood up to preach, where I could only imagine the shame he may have felt. Now let's say the events of that evening happened exactly the same way with the exception of me not preaching. Let's say I was just a visitor coming to check the church out. Do you think I would stay, even though it is one of the best churches in town where the gospel is preached faithfully? No. While one incident does not necessarily make a culture, the point is how we treat people really does matter.

The culture of the church is a powerful factor in whether people stay in a particular church and even in the universal church. This is on full display when we consider the many people of color who are deconstructing their faith. With very few exceptions, the conversations I have had with my fellow minorities all begin with some negative racial experience perpetrated by White Christians. Even more traumatic is that when some reached out to the leaders of these White or multi-ethnic churches to express their grievance, those leaders failed them either explicitly by downplaying the incident or implicitly by refusing to exercise the requisite courage to call out the sin. In any event, by their passivity or their blatant cowardice, these leaders contributed to a culture that is proving more and more hostile to minority image bearers. These are perilous times for churches aspiring to be multiethnic.

Culture is, again, the decisions we make and do not make. Culture is the product of what we proclaim and what we practice. Because the gospel is to be the most potent culture-making force in the church, how we proclaim and practice this gospel is of primary importance. The evangelical church in America has failed to live up to the biblical vision of ethnic unity because from America's inception, she has abdicated her responsibility to produce a culture of ethnic unity, both in what she proclaims and, most devastatingly, in how she has practiced the robust gospel.

PROCLAIMING A ROBUST GOSPEL

A church's understanding of the gospel is the biggest culture-making factor for that local body of Christ. For example, if a church emphasizes only the vertical dimensions of the gospel—getting people connected to God through the death, burial, and resurrection of Jesus—then it is bound to produce self-righteous Pharisees who only think of Christianity in terms of their "personal relationship with God" while not engaging others, even the ethnic other, with the love of God. What's more, this kind of culture condemns or avoids our friends in the LGBTQ+ community and accuses people of critical race theory any time the subject of race comes up.

On the other hand, if a local church only thinks of the gospel horizontally in terms of how we relate to other people, but it is detached from a vertical relationship with Christ so that he has been reduced from being our Savior to being an example, then it will not have the moral compass nor the spiritual authority to see the gospel truly transform people. This kind of church is reduced to nothing more than most modern companies, where diversity is sought after, tolerance is practiced, and the preacher is little more than the VP of human resources telling people how they should or should not relate to others. If people want to be changed, they should go to the vertical church, though they may not like what they are changed into; but if they want to be affirmed, they should go to the horizontal church. Neither is satisfying. Both are less than the biblical vision.

The Scriptures do not make a false dichotomy claiming that the gospel must be either vertical or horizontal. Instead, it's a both/and. But looking at where things stand now with the church, compared to what the Bible teaches as it relates to our relationship with God and others, something is wrong. Sure, the multiethnic church in America has grown, yet the recent data shows 78 percent of churches are still homogeneous, making the multiethnic church the outlier rather than the norm. What's more is this data is from before the traumatic turmoil of 2020, a year marked by the killings of Ahmaud Arbery, Breonna Taylor, and George Floyd, along with the controversial presidential race between Joe Biden and Donald Trump that culminated in an insurrection. Something tells me the multiethnic church is taking steps backward.

But this is long in the making. I fear the multiethnic church will recede, because while the data measures diversity, it cannot measure unity. And when it comes to race relations in the church, American evangelicals since our nation's inception, by and large, have never made an attempt at ethnic unity. The result is a legacy leaving modern day evangelicals in our nation historically impotent to address the needs of the hour.

In the 1730s and 1740s, the American colonies experienced a revival known as the Great Awakening. Many came to faith in Jesus through the preaching of evangelicals like Jonathan Edwards and George Whitefield. This revival occurred during slavery. And when the revival ended, slavery continued, never missing a beat. Toward the end of the 1700s, another revival broke out in America known as the Second Great Awakening. Many colleges, seminaries, and mission societies were founded as a result. Like the first awakening, the second took place during slavery, and when it ended, slavery was still thriving. Revival broke out again in America in 1857—the same year the Supreme Court handed down the Dred Scott decision, which would deny citizenship to African Americans —and lasted into 1859, with many coming to faith during what historians call the Businessman's Revival. But looking at these dates, we can see the revival began and ended during slavery. How does revival happen in America and yet leave the "peculiar institution" of slavery untouched? Because American evangelicalism has been historically structured along almost exclusively vertical lines, leaving no category for horizontal engagement and brotherhood with people of different ethnicities. Their doctrine was great, but their culture was wrong because their gospel was cut in half.

Around the turn of the century, in downtown Los Angeles, the Azusa Street Revival took shape. This was a truly multiethnic revival led by a Black preacher named William Seymour. Its aftershocks continue to be felt today in that it birthed the modern Pentecostal church and led to many missionaries being sent out all over the world. Cecil M. Robeck argues in his book that the ultimate demise of the revival was a power struggle in which Whites became increasingly uncomfortable following the leadership of Seymour.[1] The movement met its demise in 1908, having begun and ended under Jim Crow.

At the same time, a debate that came to be known as the fundamentalist/modernist controversy was brewing in the ecclesiological landscape of America. The seminal work during this period of controversy was written by a brilliant Presbyterian scholar named J. Gresham Machen. Uncomfortable with the swelling tide of what we would today call liberalism, Machen quit his post at Princeton Theological Seminary and ventured down to Philadelphia to form the Westminster Theological Seminary, a school devoted to the fundamentals of the faith. In 1923, Machen wrote his classic, *Christianity and Liberalism*. While an orthodox believer today would have no qualms with Machen's book, it is important to note that he does not discuss how Christianity should play out horizontally in relations with others. It really is stunning that at the height of institutionalized racial segregation, Machen offered nothing in regard to how the gospel should intersect with the ethnic others of his day who were denied the right to vote, subjected to convict leasing, and were being lynched. There just is no other way to say it: *Christianity and Liberalism*, by its silence, was complicit in aiding the machinery of Jim Crow.

What is the result of all this? A few questions should be asked: Can we really call something a "revival" or "awakening" if it refused to deal with sinful institutions, many served by the very people coming to the altar and getting "saved"? How did slavery and Jim Crow go unscathed during the awakenings and revivals of their times?

This gets to what sociologists Michael Emerson and Christian Smith point out in their important work *Divided by Faith*, in which they argue White evangelicals see sin in purely personal rather than systemic terms. This paradigm allowed the revivals and awakenings of yesteryear to be relegated to the heart and not the institutions. The obstinance continues among their progeny, as many of today's evangelicals become outraged and cry "critical race theory" when anyone suggests there are actual systems working against people of color. The refusal to acknowledge systemic injustice and sin among American evangelicals is not new. It is as old as slave-owning Jonathan Edwards and slave-lobbying George Whitefield, the two great preachers of revival.

It's been said that while history may not repeat itself, it sure does rhyme. This historical context is key because when minorities venture into White churches aspiring to be multiethnic, they are dealing with a lot of history in those seats, where the people are ill equipped to truly empathize with fellow image bearers of color. By default, the culture of these kinds of churches will be hostile to people of color in all the subtly acceptable forms of Christianity, mainly seen in turning a deaf ear to our requests.

A minority friend of mine is serving on staff at a currently homogeneous church that has gone on record saying God has called them to be multiethnic. My friend is an intentional part of their strategy. Yet after serving there for several years, he has noticed the church has not preached from the pulpit about how the gospel intersects with race. He brought this up in a meeting with the pastor, who pushed back by saying they have to be careful around sensitive topics of race and how he doesn't want to cause division. My friend reminded the pastor they also preached several times a year on money, another sensitive topic. He concluded that if ethnic unity was a value just like Christlike financial stewardship, and if both are very sensitive subjects, they should either preach on both or ignore both. But to preach on money and not race is to acknowledge you value the economics of the church more than ethnic unity.

As a reconciler, I am less concerned with diagnosing the problem and far more concerned with offering a path forward. When we speak of the necessity of a robust gospel that encompasses humanity's vertical need for God, and the need to be discipled into the new humanity known as the body of Christ populated with people from various ethnic groups, what are we to proclaim?

I am not a trained historian, but I am unashamedly committed to the Scriptures and see them as the beginning and end in informing Christian practice and shaping the culture of the church. Jesus saw the culture of the Pharisees to be at odds with the biblical vision of the kingdom of heaven empowered by the gospel. They were the original fundamentalists. They were known for their piety and obsessive obedience to the minutiae of the law. They pored over the Scriptures. They were also known for a lack of inclusivity with their rejection of the ethnic other. In Jesus' story of a Samaritan helping an individual who had been accosted and left for dead, two paragons of Judaism—a priest and a Levite— bypassed this man on their way to the temple. Distracted by their duties for God, they neglected the suffering of humanity. They loved God, just not the people made in his image.

In 1947, almost a quarter of a century after the release of Machen's book, scholar Carl F. H. Henry unleashed his classic, *The Uneasy Conscience of Modern Fundamentalism*. Henry, a White, Jesus-loving man, delivers a scathing rebuke on fundamentalists who saw the gospel in purely vertical dimensions while disregarding its horizontal mandates. The American church, he argues, is in need of a "progressive fundamentalism with a social message."[2] In a precursor to Emerson and Smith, he says one of the many problems with fundamentalism is a limited view of sin in purely personal and not social forms.[3] Then, reaching back to the imagery of Luke 10, Henry proclaims, "But what is almost wholly unintelligible to the naturalistic and idealist groups, burdened as they are for a new world order, is the lack of any social passion in Protestant Fundamentalism. On this evaluation, Fundamentalism is the modern priest and Levite, by-passing suffering humanity."[4]

We may not like terms like *social gospel*, but we cannot read our Bibles without being confronted with what Henry calls the "social imperative."[5] Let us remember, Jesus only tells the story of the Good Samaritan to answer a lawyer's question about who his neighbor is. In this context, we are forced to conclude our neighbor is everyone we meet, particularly those who have been beaten down and are suffering. To proclaim the gospel, therefore, is to proclaim its social imperative. How can any church claim to be a "gospel-centered" church and not acquiesce to the gravitational pull of the Scriptures and its over two thousand verses dealing with the poor, the widowed, the orphaned, and immigrant?

It's been said the pulpit is the steering wheel of the church, and there is much truth to this maxim. Because of the power of the stage in forming a gospel-rich culture, the message from the stage must entail an unflinching commitment to preach what the apostle Paul called the "whole counsel of God." If I have not been clear so far, let me assuage any doubt that our vertical reconciliation to God is of first importance. The culture of any church must talk freely of humanity's sin and the irreparable damage it has done to our relationship with God.

Notice I have used the word *sin*. Not issues. Not dysfunction. Not challenges. We are sinners, born, as King David said, "in sin" (Psalm 51:5). The American church, steeped in individualism, needs to understand that sin not only affects the individual but also their relationships with others. Sin is why Adam and Eve hid from God and each other. Sin is why God had to bring Cain out of darkness and into the light after he killed his brother. Sin impedes our fellowship with God and with each other (1 John 1:1-10). Sin is social.

Racism is sin. Or as Paul would write to the Galatians on Peter's racism, it is conduct "not in step with the truth of the gospel" (Galatians 2:14). The pastor of the church must call out all sin, including the sin of racism.

When one of our sons was at the hospital for a rare blood disorder, we learned a lot about white blood cells. When something is out of order in our bodies or is perceived as a threat, white blood cells go to work, confronting the issue in order to instigate health. The church is referred to as the body of Christ. I like this analogy because when anything threatens the unity of the body, the white blood cells of the congregation hold a biblical mandate to graciously confront the sin in the body, even the sin of racism. We go on the offensive. If the local church is to experience ethnic unity, we must be willing to deal with the sin of racism in the same way Jesus did—full of grace and truth.

But we are met with a challenge here. While I have spent a lot of time pointing out the deficiencies among the fundamentalists, or conservatives, I don't want anyone to think I am playing favorites. Our friends on the left are not the answer to ethnic unity either, mainly because they have made tolerance the sine qua non of our society, which means the worst thing one can be labeled today is racist. The effect of this liberal, unbiblical view is an attempt by everyone to sequester their racism and not truly express what they feel. We see this in the church through the outrage people express when they are challenged for their racism. The result is we don't talk about race or racism, which means we can never treat what we fail to diagnose.

A healthy doctrine of sin, however, says there is no such thing as being canceled. All of our sins were canceled on the cross and washed by the blood of the Lamb. When we truly embrace this, we can say with John Newton, the famous ex–slave trader, "I am a great sinner, but Christ is a great Savior." When my identity is in Christ, and not in some conservative or liberal ideology, I can be confronted on my sin, weep over my sin, and then rejoice over the grace of Jesus, which covers my sin. Now I am free to yank into the light what has been hidden in darkness, and true reconciliation can happen. This is what it means to proclaim a robust gospel.

Preaching or proclaiming a robust gospel also demands having a standard, and ours is the Word of God. This is an easy sell for American evangelicals because evangelicalism has historically acknowledged the Bible as the locus of truth. It's not as easy of a sell for our liberal or progressive friends who have a penchant for redirecting truth from the Scriptures to the experience of individuals. People used to look outside of themselves for guidance on what was right or wrong. Those days are long gone. Now people look inward for their direction, all in the name of love. Paul, in his great love chapter of 1 Corinthians 13, says love "rejoices with the truth," not "my truth" (1 Corinthians 13:6). The Bible is truth, and our commitment is to the truth of the Scriptures, meaning people must conform their lives to the Bible and not the other way around.

There is a story of a ship that was traveling one evening when it encountered a bright light shining directly in its path. Over the radio, the captain received instructions from this light to turn several degrees to the right. The captain responded he would not and told the other ship to turn several degrees to the left. Then the captain asked the captain of the other ship what his rank was. The captain of the other "ship" said that he had no rank and he was not on a ship—he was manning the lighthouse. The captain immediately changed his position. Ships adjust to what is immovable. The Word of God is our lighthouse, and we adjust our lives to the immutable nature of God and his Word, which is the same "yesterday and today and forever" (Hebrews 13:8).

Building a culture saturated with gospel nutrients begins with the primacy of Scripture, which leads us to bend the entirety of our lives to the lighthouse of God's Word. If you are vetting churches, one of the main things you should look for is preaching that privileges the Word of God. The Bible sets the agenda for the message. Sounds simple, right? But if you haven't figured it out yet, a lot of churches don't get this right and instead use the Bible as a diving board to jump off into many other topics and subjects. I am certainly not against topical preaching, and this book is not the place to argue for or against. But we need preaching that excavates the Word of God, and when a preacher makes this bold commitment, they have no choice but to deal with the "social imperative" of the ethnic other.

Some years ago, there was a commercial in which a man makes spaghetti while his father objects that he's using sauce from a jar. The father asks if the sauce has real garlic, herbs, and onions, and the son repeatedly replies, "It's in there." The message being sent is that everything needed in a sauce could be found in this particular brand.[6]

The tagline of "It's in there" is also true of the Word of God. I've been reading and preaching God's Word for decades, and I'm still astounded by all it contains. This is especially true when we think of the attention the Bible gives to the ethnic other. How can we read the book of Ruth without coming to terms with her status as an immigrant from the foreign nation of Moab? She's also a widow who ends up in a relationship with a well-to-do Jewish man and ultimately becomes the great-grandmother of King David and an ancestor of Jesus. If the Old Testament is the story of God using the people of Israel to reach the world (Genesis 12:1-3), then the multiethnic relationship of Boaz and Ruth is an unavoidable illustration of God's plan. Time doesn't permit me to discuss the multiethnic dynamics between Nebuchadnezzar and Daniel, where the most powerful king in the world is led to faith in Israel's God because of Daniel's witness. Moses marries an African woman, and God is ticked when his siblings express discomfort with their union. It's in there. How can anyone preach the Epistles without making reference to the nature of the recipients—a multiethnic community of faith? When a church gives itself to preaching the primacy of Scripture, the multiethnic nature of God's kingdom along with an emphasis of the "social imperative" become constant themes. This is what it means to preach a robust gospel.

ETHNIC UNITY DISCUSSION

What do you think of the statement, "When it comes to gospel witness, gospel culture crushes gospel doctrine"?

Have you ever heard of the phrase "just preach the gospel," and if so, how was it used?

CHAPTER SEVEN

PRACTICING A ROBUST GOSPEL

INTEGRITY CAN BE DEFINED as the alignment of words with deeds. A person full of integrity is someone you can count on when they say they will do something. There's a peace of mind that comes with a culture of integrity. Just ask kids who grew up in homes that, while not perfect, had parents who labored to fulfill the vows they made to one another and provided an atmosphere of love and security. Integrity is the best sleep aid around.

The reverse is also true. Children assume integrity on the part of their parents. It is a life-changing, traumatic moment when their assumptions are dashed. Ask any adult who grew up in a broken home. And what's true of children and homes is also true of the church.

Taking inventory of our cultural moment, we hear a lot of talk about how so-and-so has decided to "deconstruct" their faith. This is the language of the disappointed offspring of a church culture that has failed to live up to the plumb line of the Bible and as a result has shattered the assumptions of the spiritual children in the congregation. Preaching a robust gospel while failing to practice a robust gospel results in ecclesiological orphans at best; at worst, it results in people who leave the faith altogether. It bears repeating: when it comes to gospel witness, gospel culture trumps gospel doctrine. And gospel culture is more than what we say; it's how we live.

Jesus understood this. Huddled with his followers in a room overlooking the Kidron Valley, he said the insignia of their faith is love. Earlier, Jesus announced the whole law could be reduced to one word: love. Writing to the Corinthians, Paul told them their gifts must arise from love and that love is the MVP of all Christian virtues, greater than even faith and hope. Of the nine attributes of life in the Spirit, the first to be mentioned is love. If the robust gospel is both vertical and horizontal, and if the law can be reduced to loving God with the totality of our being (vertical) and our neighbor as ourselves (horizontal), then to practice a robust gospel means to love.

But this then raises the question of the precise nature of love. What does it really mean to love? Google "love" and you'll be overwhelmed by billions of hits. Query the ancient Greeks what they thought of love, and you'd get a handful of responses. According to the Greeks, one idea of love is *erōs*, from which we get words like *erotic*. Yes, sex is a theme in this form of love, but to the Greeks, *erōs* entailed more than just sex. At its core, *erōs* is intoxication. *Erōs* is what happened when my wife and I first met. Long walks on the beach. Late night talks on the phone when neither of us wanted to hang up, so we'd say, "You hang up. No, you hang up." One time—and please keep this between us—we both loved a certain R&B group. So we'd be on the phone with each other, put the CD in our respective boom boxes, and press play at the same time. That, my friend, is *erōs*.

However, there are several problems with *erōs* when we think about multiethnic relationships. In general, *erōs* is great in beginning a relationship but comes up short in sustaining a relationship. Feelings make wonderful passengers but horrible drivers, which means *erōs* needs to be in the car but never behind the wheel. And even more so, *erōs* is a finicky passenger, jumping in and out of the car whenever it pleases. *Erōs* cannot be trusted. If people of different ethnicities waited to show love to each other only when they had all the feels, there would be long stretches where they would not feel loved.

I understand for many of us there's a disconnect here. Erōs *with a church? I've never felt intoxicated with church or the people of God*, you think. Not so fast. Dietrich Bonhoeffer would object. In his classic book *Life Together*, he exposes the problem of *erōs* in the community of faith: "Those who love their dream of a Christian community more than the Christian community itself become destroyers of that Christian community even though their personal intentions may ever be so honest, earnest and sacrificial."[1] Our longing for meaningful relationships with one another inevitably leads to an ideal of what those relationships should look like. Being intoxicated with the ideal (*erōs*) both hinders and harms actual community because we become so distracted by the picture that we fail to embrace the reality.

A friend of mine was hired as a pastor at an aging homogeneous church just outside of a large urban center. During the interview process, he made it clear his passion was to see this church become multiethnic. The elders agreed. So off they went. Immediately he made staff changes and preached sermons on race, and when people began to push back, his response was to get with it or get out. In less than two years *he* was out.

As he was going over the autopsy report with me of his time as pastor at this church, I had two thoughts. One was the old saying that if a person stays one step ahead of the people, they are a leader. Two steps ahead, and they are a visionary. Three steps ahead, and they are a martyr. The other thought was Bonhoeffer's words. My friend fell more in love with the picture of what could be than with the people as they were. His intoxication with the beloved community impeded his ability to lead the people into the desired destiny. *Erōs* not only cost him his job, but it also proved inept at translating the vision into reality.

Disappointment is the chasm between what we expect and what we experience. My friend was disappointed, and chances are you have experienced some measure of disappointment when it comes to ethnic unity. The picture we have in our minds of what will be (Revelation 5:1-10), compared to the reality of what is, may be disappointing. Let us resolve to not love pictures more than people. Let us be immovable in our commitment to embrace who we are as we journey into who we will become.

Jesus doesn't say all people will know we are followers of his by our *erōs* for one another, nor does he say by our *phileō* of one another. *Phileō* is another Greek word for love, and it is really the idea of friendship. I'm from Philadelphia, which gets its name from this Greek word. While I love the city of my birth, it's so not named properly. Just ask Ben Simmons, a former athlete who played professionally in Philadelphia. When the City of Brotherly Love fans perceived he was not trying his hardest on the court, they didn't show him much *phileō*.

Phileō is friendship. It is the kind of relationship that begins on a note of affinity or connection. This is what C. S. Lewis was getting at when he said all friendship begins with "oh, you too." *Phileō* is "I like you. We have things in common." It's telling that Jesus does not use this word to detail how his followers are to relate to one another and the world. He knew the nature of the kingdom expressed through the local church would encompass people from all walks of life, and if the currency of love demanded affinity, the church would be propelled downward into homogeneity.

The average first-century church had around thirty people and met in a home. The church would have comprised the owner of the home with his family and several slaves. If there were tenants in the home, they likely would have taken part. Several poor people, along with former female prostitutes, would have participated as well. And of course, there would be Jews, who grew up very religious and moral.[2] With a group so economically, culturally, and ethnically diverse, there was no way *phileō* would prove strong enough to sustain this "fellowship of differents." The only thing that could hold them together was *agapē*, the third major Greek term for love.

Agapē is acting for the best interest of others regardless of how you or they feel. Unlike *erōs*, *agapē* is a steeled commitment. And unlike *phileō*, *agapē* transcends a feeling of mutuality, engaging even those who act hostile toward you.

The poet Robert Frost goes on about how home is the place where they have to let you in. Don't we know it. While I have some family members I feel *phileō* with, there are others I do not. But when the latter has needed anything, I've done my best to be there to help. We've never turned our backs on each other. Every year we show up several times to events, where we laugh, reminisce, and at times even cry together. We confide. We call. We confront. We apologize. We look out for. I certainly don't feel intoxicated with them, and with some, I'm sure if we didn't share DNA we wouldn't relate to one another the way we have. But we, a "fellowship of differents," are family. We let each other in. The force that keeps us together is *agapē*.

To practice a robust gospel means to put *agapē* on display. *Agapē* really pops against the contrast of ethnic differences. Like a diamond against the backdrop of a black velvet cloth, the love of Christ dazzles the world against the backdrop of the multiethnic church—a church that lets each other in because we are family.

If you've been to a wedding, chances are you have heard the famous love chapter 1 Corinthians 13 read with all its descriptors of love while the bride and groom exude *erōs*. By the time Paul's exhortation ends, we feel overwhelmed. There's no way we can love like this, which is Paul's point. This is why love is personified as a Person and why, later on to the Galatians, *agapē* is linked to the Holy Spirit. None of us are able to have *agapē*; rather, it is the work of the Holy Spirit borne through our yielded lives. So, a church that practices a robust gospel rife with love is also a church that has a high view of the Holy Spirit, giving him room in the life of the individual and collective groups of people to do what we cannot do on our own.

In the early days of the Azusa Street Revival, a White minister from North Carolina boarded a train to see if what he had read was true. Among the people of God, he was struck by the multiethnic gathering led by the Black minister William Seymour. He also sensed a move of the Holy Spirit, and he began to pray. While in prayer he felt a hand on his shoulder. Opening his eyes, this White minister from the Jim Crow South was astonished to see a Black man praying for him. His presuppositions and cultural norms were being shattered. Around the same time, a reporter for the *Los Angeles Times* put into words what this White minister felt by writing of how the color line was washed away at Azusa Street. William Seymour's summation proves far more poignant: "Pentecost makes us love Jesus more, and our brothers more. It brings us into one common family."[3] Seymour uses "Pentecost" to refer to the work of the Holy Spirit. And what does this work give birth to? Love.

What people experienced well over a century ago on Azusa Street was the work of the Holy Spirit and a kind of *agapē* love that transgressed cultural norms and ethnic lines. We mortals cannot bring this about. But Christ can and already has, when he used the cross as a sledgehammer to shatter the dividing wall of hostility (Ephesians 2). All we must do is lean into the Spirit and walk in what has already been achieved.

LEARN

But what does this mean? My friend Matt Chandler, pastor of the Village Church in Flower Mound, Texas, says their pursuit of what he calls "ethnic harmony" has led them to make three commitments: to be a community that learns, laments, and lives together.[4] When a local body of Christ-followers gives themselves to these three pursuits, they are exuding an otherworldly, *agapē* kind of love.

To love anyone is to embark on an adventure of discovery. One way to gauge the seriousness of a relationship is the moment you realize it's time to take them home to meet your family of origin. It is here where we learn embarrassing nicknames and anecdotes about each other. It's also here where we collect information about more sobering realities and gain a fuller context for who the other is, allowing us to understand and love one another more.

Every other month I gather with our Asian members from the church to enjoy a meal and to learn. We talk about Lunar New Year and its significance. The older ones speak of their experience as first-generation immigrants to our country and the pain they had to endure. Their children talk about the message they received from their parents about the importance of hard work and being successful. They also talk of the silent pressure the Black/White binary presents. Which side will they choose, if at all? All of this is so new to me. It feels as if I have nothing to offer but my ears, yet afterward I am always inundated with calls and emails telling me how grateful they are for the opportunity. My presence matters.

When I was fresh out of seminary and serving in my first pastorate, I was called on to visit people in the hospital, which meant I made the rookie mistake of barging into rooms spewing Bible verses, ready to fix the pain and provide answers. Through much trial and error, along with facing scenarios I realized my studies failed to equip me to handle, I learned these dear people were not looking for answers as much as they were for comfort, and comfort is spelled p-r-e-s-e-n-c-e. Ask Job. His friends were at their finest the first week when they sat there in the ashes with him and said nothing. The moment they attempted to provide answers, things went south. So over time, I have learned to sit with people, ask questions, offer a word of prayer, and leave. It's uncanny—every time I exit the hospital parking lot, I have learned far more than I have taught. I think this is what Solomon was alluding to when he wrote, "It is better to go to the house of mourning than to go to the house of feasting" (Ecclesiastes 7:2).

This odyssey in learning is important, because the table for multiethnic education is often set during times of pain and suffering. In these moments, a part of the family of God finds themselves in the "house of mourning." And what we don't need is another part of the family barging in with their answers and warnings against critical race theory. Why don't we try sitting with one another and genuinely asking questions in an effort to understand? When we listen, we learn.

If you are a preacher, you should aspire to quote widely during your sermons. When you quote cross-ethnically, you have no idea the sense of joy you will instill in people because you have taken the time to listen and learn. If you are a follower of Jesus with a healthy doctrine of the church, this should lead you to seek to learn about all kinds of people, particularly the ones who are in your region. We should be reading historical pieces on the civil rights movement, like Taylor Branch's definitive trilogy. We should learn about our Asian American siblings by watching documentaries such as the PBS five-hour film special *Asian Americans*. Make it your aim to read rich theology from scholars of color, like Cuban American theologian Justo Gonzalez's wonderful *The Story of Christianity*. I am glad you are reading this book on the multiethnic church, but it is just one resource on a growing list that includes all kinds of ethnicities and various genders. Visit museums that will broaden your understanding of history, listen to podcasts on the multiethnic church (I have one called *The Kainos Podcast*[5]), and simply ask questions. As much as you can, do these things in community with other Christ-followers. This is what we do at our church. At least once a month, we take some of our staff to a local museum on slavery where we embark on a ninety-minute guided tour, followed by a meal so we can process together what we experienced and how we are feeling. We are committed to learning together.

LAMENT

We love practically when we not only commit to learn across the ethnic divide but also when we lament with one another. Writing to the Romans, Paul instructs them to "weep with those who weep" (Romans 12:15). He is calling the church to engage in the practice of lament.

Lament is hard for many of us for several reasons. In his book *Prophetic Lament*, Soong-Chan Rah points out that the overwhelming majority of our worship songs are triumphalist. We sing about a Jesus who conquered the grave and will return and a God who gives us amazing grace. Rah also reveals that a tiny portion of what we sing is lament focused. What this means is we are constructing a culture that does not know how to sit in the ashes with those who have been devastated by life. We don't know how to lament with one another.

The practice of lament is awkward also because, unlike anything else, it strikes against our individualism and forces us outside of ourselves to connect with the hurting. To weep with those who weep is about the most un-American thing we can do. Actually, scratch that—to mourn with another ethnicity whose mourning is birthed out of an ethnic-specific tragedy is *the* most un-American thing to do. It forces us to not only come outside of ourselves but to also connect with someone of another ethnicity, thus putting us at odds with what has been called our country's original sin.

Still others consider lament a challenge because they think to enter into this practice is to assume culpability for what happened. However, weeping with someone over the killing of a minority at the hands of a White police officer does not mean you are rendering a verdict of guilt. Instead, your lament is a confession of availability that whispers, "I am here. I am with you," even when you don't know all of the facts.

This works the other way as well. I was once in a meeting with a dozen or so police officers from our church who were mostly White. The meeting was convened right on the heels of a string of deaths of people of color at the hands of the police. I nor the other pastors from our church said much in the meeting. With tears, the officers shared how they felt the media attention was placing their lives at risk. Before all of this they would have been more decisive, but now they hesitated, thus endangering themselves. As a Black man I silently nursed my share of defenses and retorts. But Paul's words to the Romans came to mind: "weep with those who weep." Now was not the time to get into the forensics of each case the national media shined a spotlight on. Instead, I entered in, allowing myself to feel the emotions of the moment. My lament was not an agreement with the so-called facts of each case but an alignment to their feelings. These were my brothers and sisters in pain.

I now preach and think differently about collisions between police and people of color because I no longer see only badges and uniforms but tears, faces, and hearts. There really is something special about coming out from behind the biased media of our TVs to sit in a room with one another.

Churches must build a culture of lament. We need to steep in the psalms of lament. We need to become familiar with the

Black gospel tradition, which is filled with songs of lament. Yes, we should plan our services and use helpful tools like Planning Center, but remember, they are only tools. We should have moments to grieve over the way our Asian siblings have been treated during the pandemic, to grieve the latest killing of people of color at the hands of the police, to grieve with officers whose lives are endangered. Communal lament is one of the most helpful things we can do in our journey into ethnic unity because it reminds us we are connected to one another.

LIVE

How do we know we are practicing a robust gospel filled with *agapē*? We not only learn and lament together, we also live together. No, I am not saying you should sell your home and literally move into the church. I am advocating for a deep commitment to one another, a kind of commitment that says we are in this together, rain or shine.

To understand this, we must see the church as one of three institutions God has created for human flourishing. The first institution God established was family, followed by government and finally the church. When a man and woman come together in the covenant of marriage, they make vows to one another. They commit. Many government positions have a swearing in ceremony where promises are given. They commit. And for the longest time, the people of God in the local church committed to one another. In Acts 2, Luke observes that the church was "devoted" and that this devotion led them to sell their possessions and give to those in need (Acts 2:42-47). A few chapters later, Luke writes that they were so committed to each other they had "everything in common" and "there was not a needy person among them" (Acts 4:32, 34). Stories in church history abound of believers' commitment to one another. It was common for a poor person to come to a local church, and when word got out that they didn't have food, the other believers, if they didn't have extra food, would fast and give up the little they had so the other could eat. That's commitment. That's what it means to live together.

We don't often see this kind of commitment and devotion to one another in local churches today. Sure, we catch glimpses of it and are astounded because honestly, they are so outside the norm. What is normal is to see followers of Jesus leave the church for the most trivial of reasons. People leave because they don't like the style of preaching. Or they found a better student ministry down the street and around the corner. Or the style of singing is not to their liking. On and on it goes, and I'm just getting started. I once got a note from someone in our church complaining about one of our campus pastors who had the "nerve" to say University of North Carolina fans should show some grace over their recent victory over Duke University. This needed to be fixed or they were leaving. Seriously. Granted, this campus pastor was new and had no idea how intense this basketball rivalry is, but I'm going to go out on a limb and say if you'll leave over something like that, I don't have much confidence you will lay down your life for Jesus. And of course, if you ever worry about too many people coming to your church, I know what you can do to immediately create space. That's right: preach on race, or be perceived as either saying the wrong thing or not enough about race.

I fielded many calls during the Covid-19 pandemic over churches that were hemorrhaging people because of the race conversation. Many Whites in these churches left because the pastor had turned "woke" or gone "critical race theory." On the other hand, many minorities who left did so because the pastor had not said enough or said the wrong thing in their estimation. We don't really know what it means to live together in deep commitment as a local body of Christ. So, what are we to do?

The church at Corinth was a multiethnic one made up of Jews and Greeks. They were—how shall I say this—a hot mess. They were using the Lord's Supper as a time to entrench division and class lines. They were at each other's throats over whether they could eat certain types of food. One dude was sleeping with his stepmother. And the Corinthians were using the spiritual gifts God had given them for building up others to instead shine a spotlight on themselves. Yes, they were a hot mess. If ever there was a church one wanted to tap out on, it was the church at Corinth. But in Paul's opening words to the church he says something astounding: "I give thanks to my God always for you" (1 Corinthians 1:4). Really?

Quick story. At the end of my sister's seventh grade year, my parents got called up to the school for an impromptu meeting. You know how everybody signs each other's yearbooks on the last day? Well, I guess one particular girl was on my sister's last nerve and didn't know it, and she asked my sister to sign her yearbook. When the teacher caught wind of what my sister inscribed, she reached out to my parents, who were horrified. Now, I'm a follower of Jesus writing a book on the church, so I won't tell you exactly what she said, but it went something like this: "Have a wonderful summer, female dog. Signed [my sister's name]."

Kudos to my sister for assuming responsibility by putting her name next to the expletive. This either makes her courageous or ditzy. Whatever the case, I can guarantee you the only person my parents thanked was the teacher. I could not imagine, given my sister's behavior, my parents saying anything in that moment to the effect of, "I give thanks to my God always for you."

Yet, while those words did not come out of my folks' mouths, their actions were congruent with Paul's. Both refused to tap out on their relationship. Instead, they doubled down. Paul thanking God for the Corinthians in spite of their awful behavior was him communicating his commitment to them. To Paul, the church was not a sorority or fraternity filled with pledges who had to perform well to make it in. It was a community of what Brennan Manning calls "ragamuffins" in need of deep grace. This is why Paul, right on the heels of giving thanks for the Corinthians, explains why: "because of the grace of God that was given you in Christ Jesus" (1:4). Paul doubled down on his commitment to this undeserving church because they had received grace from God.

There's a psychiatric principle called fundamental attribution error. When I make a mistake I attribute it to circumstances, but when I see you make a mistake, I chalk it up to your character. Let's say I'm late for work one day. It's because my wife and I had an argument that morning and I ran into traffic. But when I see you walk into the office late, it's because you are lazy and irresponsible. At its core, fundamental attribution error says humans are promiscuous when heaping grace on themselves and celibate when extending grace to others. So your pastor didn't get it right when it came to what they did or did not say about the racially charged moment in our culture. Gracious people don't just up and leave. We sit down and have a conversation. We pray for the pastor. Sure, there is a time to leave, but let's be slow to look for the exits because we are all in process.

This is Paul's point in 1 Corinthians 1:2 when he says, "To the church of God that is in Corinth, to those *sanctified* in Christ Jesus" (emphasis mine). To be sanctified means to be set apart. Remember your grandmother's china cabinet? You don't put 7-Eleven Big Gulp cups in china cabinets, oh no. China cabinets are where you put the special stuff, the stuff set apart for Sunday dinners and special guests. Paul tells the church at Corinth that when they were saved, God set them apart. They are special and different, not because of their own works but because of the work of God through Christ. As a result, the church of God is to look different, uncommon. This is what it means to be sanctified.

But there's more. Sanctification is the process by which God is making us to be what he has already declared us to be: holy. We are all in process—a process that will not culminate until we are given our new glorified body and behold our Lord and Savior face to face. So, a healthy theology of sanctification acknowledges the process, and this sets the table for patience.

I have a friend whose wife died. Sometime later he got into the world of online dating. I checked in with him to see how it was going, and he sounded frustrated. "I meet these nice ladies online and show up to coffee with them, but Bryan, they look nothing like their picture." (And we know the same can be said of men.) Spiritually, that's all of us, isn't it? We look nothing like what we will be when we get to heaven. That's why I love the song we used to sing in our little church growing up: "Please be patient with me, God is not through with me yet." That's some good sanctification theology right there!

What does this mean for us and our commitment to live together in the multiethnic church? It means everything. A healthy theology of sanctification means when people get it wrong and sin, I don't just up and look for the exits. When racism rears its ugly head in the church of Jesus Christ, I don't turn to cancel culture. How could I when *all* of my sins and yours have been washed by the blood of Christ and canceled on the cross? When we really understand this, we are positioned to be patient and live with *agapē* across the ethnic divide, reaching the shoreline of ethnic unity.

I've had the joy of serving as lead pastor to two thriving multiethnic churches where the culture was saturated with a robust gospel and a commitment among the people to practice it. As we were growing in our love for one another across the racial divide, we also continued to grow in diversity. What blew me away is that at some point this culture became the main "advertisement" for our church, as we were getting a reputation for ethnic unity. It wasn't my preaching—though that did play a part—but more potent was our love for one another. I know firsthand the explosive power of the gospel when it takes root in the hearts and lives of a community of Christ-followers who hold fast to Jesus and to one another.

ETHNIC UNITY DISCUSSION

When it comes to ethnic unity, in what ways can your gospel culture be better?

What are some practical ways your group can learn more about each other's unique ethnic and cultural histories?

CHAPTER EIGHT

RELIABLE LEADERSHIP

IN SEPTEMBER OF 1957, Dorothy "Dot" Counts became the first African American to integrate into Harding High School in Charlotte, North Carolina. What awaited her that day was an onslaught of hatred and vitriol that she had never experienced before. A local paper, *The Charlotte Observer*, revealed her horrified countenance to the world. She would only last four days at Harding before deciding to drop out.[1]

The prolific writer James Baldwin was moved by Dot's face in the *Charlotte Observer*. Born in Harlem, New York, Baldwin felt deeply the collective pain of the Black experience in America. In time that pain became too much, and he left the country for Paris, where he could live in relative freedom. On a fall afternoon in a Paris café, he was introduced to the travails of Dot Counts. He would go on to reflect:

> Facing us on every newspaper kiosk on that wide, tree shaded boulevard, were photographs of fifteen-year-old Dorothy Counts being reviled and spat upon by the mob as she was making her way to school in Charlotte, North Carolina. There were unutterable pride, tension and

anguish in that girl's face. . . . It made me furious, it filled me with both hatred and pity, and it made me ashamed. Some one of us should have been there with her! I dawdled in Europe for nearly yet another year, held by my private life and my attempt to finish a novel, but it was on that bright afternoon that I knew I was leaving France. I could, simply, no longer sit around in Paris discussing the Algerian and the black American problem. Everybody else was paying their dues, and it was time I went home and paid mine.[2]

Baldwin would indeed leave Paris and head back to America, where the struggle for civil rights was beginning to crest. If Martin Luther King Jr. was the voice of the movement, Baldwin became its pen. Some six years after Dorothy's brief tenure at Harding High School, Baldwin reached into his soul and spilled out all his rage and pain into a book called *The Fire Next Time*. It's impossible to articulate the impact this book and subsequent writings of his had on our nation. James would go on to lecture, debate, write, and advocate on behalf of equal rights, all because he made the costly decision to leave the safety of Paris and serve as a leader in the struggle.

We have been talking about what it takes to play offense as a church in the area of ethnic unity. Yes, we must be committed to a robust gospel, but we also must have reliable leaders who will courageously leave the "Paris" of their comfort and familiarity to engage in the struggle for our future eternal multiethnic reality in the here and now.

There are too many people in "Paris" peering over their lattes and tweeting about all that's wrong with race relations when they are not personally invested in the fight. It's easy to be a social media warrior in Paris. It's easy to podcast about the problems from Paris. And it takes no courage to tell people to leave the fight for the multiethnic church from the comforts of one's homogeneous Paris. Staying in Paris is easy and comfortable. Coming to America in the hopes of being a part of the solution takes courage and vulnerability.

THE COST—LOSING PEOPLE AND MONEY

Baldwin understood a fundamental principle of leadership: while critique may come from the outside, reform comes from within. Anybody can pontificate on the problems in America from the safety of a café in Paris. But if you really want to see change, at some point you must put the latte down, roll up your sleeves, and fight. There's a cost to leadership.

Jesus himself said, "For which of you, desiring to build a tower, does not first sit down and count the cost, whether he has enough to complete it?" (Luke 14:28). Anything of signifi-cance has a cost. And doing things of eternal value is even costlier, like building a multiethnic church. There are a lot of people who agree wholeheartedly with the vision of ethnic unity. They would say it's right and it's biblical. They will stand on stages and say with winsome boldness how God has called the church to be diverse. They will even contract people like me to come out and consult. So I pack my bags, board an airplane, and spend a few days with their team. I'll then collect my check and return home. Over dinner my wife will ask me about my time at said church, and I will say wonderful things about the people and hospitality. Then she'll widen her eyes and tilt her head as if to say, "So . . . do you think they will do what's necessary to bring about change?" Most of the time she already knows the answer. It's a rhetorical question. I'll shake my head.

Any church aspiring to play offense when it comes to race must especially count the cost. Before people sit down to build their "tower" of a multiethnic church, they should consider that they will probably lose people and money. And if they really want to build the tower right, they will lose a modicum of power.

A vision will never come to fruition without courage. Anyone can talk about vision and get people riled up, ready to charge the hill. But when you are looking at the real possibility of losing nickels and noses, that's a different thing altogether.

My years of helping churches become multiethnic has convinced me the number one question a leader must ask from the outset is, "Do we want to be big, or do we want to be multiethnic?" More times than not, these things are antonyms rather than synonyms. The question of mega or multiethnic is particularly germane if you are an existing church looking to transition into a diverse one.

Congregants tend to think of churches as if they are pictures when they are more like movies. They see their church as a still shot of its best moments, with every other iteration evaluated in comparison to their picture. But churches are films—a succession of scenes that change from time to time. When a new scene comes along people will inevitably leave, and on their way out the door they'll say something to the effect of, "This is not what I signed up for." Change locations, count on losing some people. Change pastors, count on losing some people. Change the style of music, count on losing some people. Change denominations . . . you get the point. And if you decide to fiddle with the racial demographics within a local body of believers, you can count on losing a lot of people. It's just the way things are.

A White pastor friend of mine was recently convinced God wanted him to move the church in a multiethnic trajectory. He did all the right things and proceeded at the right pace. He was gentle with the people when he was inundated with requests for meetings. Unlike my previously mentioned friend who moved three steps ahead of the congregation and thus became a martyr, this pastor stayed a step-and-a-half ahead of the people as both a leader and visionary. He did everything he could to shepherd them with patience. But despite all this, when the music and leadership started to change, people headed for the exits. When the dust settled, half the church had evaporated.

I know of another church that decided to hire the first pastor of another race in their history. Right before they made the decision, they convened an elders meeting. Everyone was on board but one elder. He said he couldn't do it, something about not liking the potential new pastor's preaching style. The other leaders knew this was a sham. They pleaded with him, but he dug in. He said if they made the decision to hire this pastor, he would have no choice but to leave. The other leaders knew this would be a costly decision—his giving alone accounted for over a third of the annual budget. Convinced they were making the right decision, these leaders wished this man well. They parted ways.

It's not just leaders who pay a price; every person of color who joins a majority White church pays as well. Church for minorities tends to be far more than a service where we sing a few songs, hear a message, give some money, and leave. In the minority experience, our churches of origin represent a rich cultural moment, where the fullness of our imago Dei is affirmed weekly through language, customs, and music. To give this up to join a majority White church is more than an exchange of churches; it is to leave a piece of us behind.

So, imagine the excitement among people of color who are minorities at a given church when the pastor shares the vision of being diverse. Something in us inches forward while something else pulls us back, not wanting to get our hopes up too high. But it's too late. The cat is out of the bag, and the vision has been cast. What we don't realize is what is as palpable as our anticipation is fear in others. This isn't the picture of the church they had taken. Little do we know in the weeks and months to come, the leadership will be inundated with calls, emails, and meetings, all saying some version of how they should just stay in Paris by preaching the gospel and not get distracted by the race stuff. The pressure on the leadership has escalated.

Now the leadership is in a real bind. To continue forward down the path of ethnic unity is to lose many in the status quo. But to acquiesce to the demands of the status quo is to lose many minorities. Or to say it another way, there's a cost to staying in Paris, and there's a cost to coming to America.

I think you and I know what typically happens in these scenarios. I'm more interested in addressing the question of why. Why do leaders so often choose to pacify the demands of the status quo and play it safe by moonwalking away from the vision of ethnic unity? I don't have any empirical evidence to offer, only a well-educated guess: economics.

If we are talking about a majority White church that has cast the vision for ethnic unity and then gets pushback from people—who are often well-resourced and also White—it is no secret why the status quo consistently wins. Money plays a bigger role in our decision making than we would like to admit. And when we talk about becoming a multiethnic church we are of course talking about race, and when we deal with race we by default run into economics. The two are kindred.

Of course, I am not saying all White people are wealthy and all minorities are not. I am acknowledging something that has plenty of empirical evidence: a significant wealth gap exists between Whites and people of color, especially Blacks. From a purely business perspective, it's not good for the budget to be multiethnic. But from a kingdom perspective, nothing can be further from the truth.

Reliable leaders in the multiethnic church are guided by the economics of the kingdom and not the economics of this world. These kinds of leaders really believe the God they serve owns the cattle on a thousand hills, and he is their source while people are their resource—the means through which God provides. So when people leave, taking their wallets with them, the leader continues to move forward, trusting God's provision. This is hard, but leadership is for grown folks, it really is true.

Remember the story I shared about the elder who contributed over a third of the budget to their church, but left because the team decided to hire a person of a different ethnicity? Well, the church finished that year in the black. When their resource left, God, their source, continued to meet their needs.

COST—LOSING POWER

There is also the cost of power. To build a multiethnic church the right way, minorities must be vested with power. Churches that authentically pursue ethnic unity are not content with diverse faces on their website; instead, they empower diverse voices on the stage and around the table of decision making. Reliable leaders understand a face without a voice is a token. For a leader to endow others with this kind of power means they are willing to divest themselves of power. But the paradox is these kinds of leaders lose nothing; instead, they gain everything.

I talk a lot about South Africa and their journey through apartheid not only because there are a lot of similarities with America's experience with slavery and Jim Crow, but also because there is much my country can learn from them. For instance, F. W. de Klerk was a courageous, reliable White leader who risked everything to dismantle apartheid. What people tend to forget is while Blacks represent a small minority in America, they are the majority in South Africa. So, for President de Klerk to put an end to apartheid was for him to pronounce the eulogy on White power and empower Blacks and people of color all at once. Think about that for a moment. He knew this decision would mean his legacy was one of ending Afrikaner hegemony, resulting in him losing his job and being denounced as an ethnic traitor by his own people. It would also, and more painfully so, set him in direct opposition to his own father, who had labored in his political career to keep apartheid in place.[3] Undeterred, de Klerk plowed forward. He released Mandela and negotiated with the African National Congress. And when the wheels were set in motion for the dissolution of apartheid, he didn't ride off into the sunset. No, he stayed and worked with Black leaders on what the new constitution for South Africa would be—a constitution that would lessen the power of his race.

What fueled all of this for de Klerk? What was the impetus for such courageous, reliable leadership? His faith in God as a devout follower of Jesus and a member of the Dutch Reformed Church in South Africa. De Klerk's brother recalls a time they went to service together at the apex of de Klerk's wrestling over the decision to end apartheid:

> "He was literally in tears after the service," his brother remembered. "In tears he told us we should pray for him—that God was calling him to save all the people of South Africa, that he was going to be rejected by his own people but that he had to walk this road and that we must all help him. He got very emotional, confessing his belief that God had called upon him and that he couldn't ignore the call. I remember, too, that he said, 'I am not a fundamentalist, I don't think I am important in God's eyes, but I believe in God and I believe I am being called to perform a specific task at this time in this new situation.'"[4]

President F. W. de Klerk was not governed by what was convenient for him or his ethnicity. Nor did he make decisions under the tyranny of people's opinions. He was a man of great faith and biblical conviction. He also happened to be White and in power but gave it all up for a greater vision. In the end, he lost nothing of eternal value but gained everything.

Like de Klerk, the leaders of the first church gave power away to minority leaders. The church's first major crisis occurred when widows who happened to be Hellenistic Jews were being overlooked for the daily distribution of food (Acts 6:1). The Jewish apostles decided to form a team of leaders and empower them to remedy this situation. The men who were chosen were Greek. The result was unity.

No leader who aspires to be multiethnic can be taken seriously if they do not consistently share the weekend preaching and teaching moments with minorities who represent the ethnicities they are trying to engage. Nor does the vision of ethnic unity have any teeth if there is not diversity around the decision-making table. By this, I mean not just diverse faces but empowered voices that have been greenlighted to play a significant role in steering the church toward its desired destination.

I don't know what drove you to read this book, but if you have been encouraged by my ministry, you have a White leader named Dr. Gordon Kirk to thank (among several others). When I was a young man in my midtwenties and days out of graduate school, Dr. Kirk hired me and put me up to preach. After my first sermon, he did the unthinkable—he said he wanted to form a teaching team for the first time in the history of the church. I don't know all the reasons for this, to be honest. He never announced a vision to be multiethnic, although I'd guess it was a part of his thinking. We preached together on Easter Sunday, and he let me share key messages in series. When I glance at the rearview of my life, I have Dr. Kirk to thank. I am where I am today because someone provided me with opportunities I had not earned. He was willing to divest himself of power, and in the end, he lost nothing but gained everything.

RELIABLE LEADERS HAVE MULTIETHNIC FRIENDSHIPS

We've talked some about the challenges facing leaders who aspire to have a multiethnic church or organization, but I also want to talk about the DNA of a reliable multiethnic leader.

What are some of the essential traits of a reliable leader who builds an offensive multiethnic church? It's here where Acts 10 is vital.

Acts 10 has been called the Gentile Pentecost because at the end of the chapter Peter, a Jew, preaches the gospel in the home of Cornelius, a centurion. Just like on the day of Pentecost, when Peter preached in Jerusalem and saw the Holy Spirit being poured out on the audience, the Holy Spirit comes on the Gentiles as Peter preaches in Acts 10.

It's no small thing that Jewish Peter would be in a Gentile home. His very presence there broke all the cultural norms instilled in him during his Orthodox Jewish upbringing. So, what did God do to get Peter to go? Well, the first thing he did was place Peter in a multiethnic relationship. Acts 9 ends by saying, "And he stayed in Joppa for many days with one Simon, a tanner" (Acts 9:43). Because Simon was a tanner (someone who worked with dead animals), he was likely not Jewish. Thus, the setting for Acts 10 is Peter doing life with a non-Jew. Here's the principle: *before God calls Peter to preach cross-ethnically, he calls him to live cross-ethnically*.

Now I know what you sophisticated theologians are thinking: Acts is not prescriptive but descriptive. Luke is just making some historical observations and not necessarily telling us how we must do things, you argue. This brings us to a major point in Bible interpretation: always take the findings of one passage and see if there is support from others. When we do this, our point is strengthened. Just look at the life of Paul. Paul, the great planter of multiethnic churches, had multiethnic friendships. He explicitly says this in 1 Corinthians 9:19-23. What's more is he was thrown in jail for the last time because he was falsely accused of taking his Greek friend Trophimus into the forbidden parts of the temple. Paul didn't just preach cross-ethnically, he lived cross-ethnically.

Leadership 101 says I can't authentically lead people to a place I'm not traveling to myself. If I want to build a rich culture of evangelism in my church or organization, I should be sharing my faith. If I have a vision to see as many people as possible go on a short-term missions trip, as the leader I should go on a few myself. And if I really understand people still come to church out of relationships with others, then sanctuaries reflect dinner tables, so I must have a diverse dinner table as a leader. Leaders, by way of life, must always be the chief shareholder of the vision.

I never stop being amazed at how many leaders just don't get this when it comes to ethnic unity. When God births a vision in your heart for this, the first thing you should do is seek relationships with the ethnic other. The reading list can wait. So can the conference and trip to the museum. You need a Trophimus, a Simon the Tanner, as a necessary part of your formation.

Why? There are several reasons. One is that God primarily forms us through relationship with him and others. The phrase "one another" is repeated more than one hundred times in the New Testament. Second, we need cross-ethnic friendships because they authenticate our vision casting. What would you think of me if I pleaded with my church to share their faith and I haven't done it? Or if I went on a very biblical rant about the importance of making disciples, but I haven't done it myself? You'd think I was a phony, and you'd be right. And if I went on and on about the beauty of the multiethnic church, but I didn't have multiethnic relation-ships, you would be just as right to think I was a hypocrite.

But there's another reason. The old preachers used to say sin dulls your preaching edge, and it really does. But the reverse is also true—holiness sharpens it. When I venture into the very thing I am casting a vision about, there is an added richness and sweetness to my preaching and leadership that connects me to the people I lead. It's what the Greeks called *ethos*, or what we call ethics or integrity. To the Greeks, a speaker had *ethos* when the audience could sense they were living what they were talking about. The best kind of leading is living.

For those of you who are at a loss in this area of cross-ethnic relationships, I would encourage you to connect with ethnically other leaders who occupy your same position at another church. Don't send someone on your team to make the connection for you. In fact, this is where many well-intentioned White leaders miss the mark when they seek to partner with minority churches in an effort to care for the community. These partnerships are beautiful but are often short-lived for several reasons. African Americans, Asian Americans, and Latinos tend to have honor cultures. The White church, oblivious to the cultural dynamics at play, often sends their outreach pastor to meet with the minority senior pastor. This is the equivalent of the White church sending lieutenants to meet with the minority church's generals, which comes across as dishonoring and offensive. If White churches want to establish a relationship with another church, the senior leader needs to connect with their senior leader.

RELIABLE LEADERS HEAR FROM GOD

While staying at the home of Simon the Tanner, Peter goes up on the roof to pray at noon. While he is in prayer, God gives him a vision of a sheet with all kinds of animals and greenlights Peter to kill and eat them. Peter responds that he can't because these animals are common or unclean. Hindsight being what it is, we understand God is setting Peter up. At the end of the chapter, Peter is in the home of another person he considers to be "common" or "unclean." God then rebukes Peter by saying, "What God has made clean, do not call common" (Acts 10:15). This is a classic a fortiori argument—an argument from lesser to greater. In other words, if God's prohibition of calling something common or unclean applies to lesser things like food, how much more will it apply to greater things like people? Peter is being prepared to take the gospel, as a Jew, to people he had been raised to consider common or unclean. One encounter with God completely changed the trajectory of his ministry.

The greatest thing leaders bring to the table is not their vision or strategy, nor is it their gifts of speaking or educational résumé. It is their walk with God. What changed Peter and resulted in many Gentiles coming to faith in Jesus was prayer.

But there's more. I believe God is still in the business of speaking to people through visions (like the one Peter had in Acts 10), prophetic words, and his still small voice. However, God has already spoken through his Word, and whatever other words I may claim to have received from him must always be measured by the Scriptures. God has already told us his plan for the church. He wants us to proclaim the kingdom by calling people to repent of their sins and come to faith in Jesus and meeting their physical needs. This is what Jesus did when he brought the kingdom. He wants us to see as many people come to faith in him in our given ministry context as possible.

What this means is if your church is in a diverse community or region, you don't have to pray about whether your church should be diverse. No special prophetic words are needed. No need to fast for a vision from God. When Paul walks into a town to preach the gospel, he wants to see the whole town come to faith in Jesus. The question whether you are called to lead a multiethnic church is not the right question. Instead, you should ask if the community is multiethnic. If the answer is yes, then I can say with biblical confidence you are called to lead a multiethnic church.

RELIABLE LEADERS ARE PEOPLE OF FAITH

After hearing from God, Peter doesn't quite get it. This is not an a-ha moment for him, which kind of makes sense. If you remember anything about Peter and the disciples during Jesus' earthly ministry, you know they were not good at deciphering the words of Jesus, particularly the parables. Once again, our boy is stumped. Humorously, Luke notes that God gives Peter this vision several more times, and then writes, "Peter was inwardly perplexed as to what the vision that he had seen might mean" (Acts 10:17). Peter's reaction is like mine when I look at the instructions to put something together from IKEA—he just doesn't get it.

Men from the house of Cornelius then show up. Luke notes that "Peter was pondering the vision" (Acts 10:19). Finally, God sends the Spirit, who tells him in clear language he is to go with these men, so "the next day he rose and went away with them" (Acts 10:23). Don't you see? Peter goes, though there's no hint he has understood the intricacies of what God was saying to him. He goes even though he has questions. He goes even though he hasn't figured it all out. He goes.

You know what we call what Peter did? Faith. Faith is not certainty. Quite the opposite. Faith presupposes risk. Faith necessitates questions. Faith settles into the possibility of losing people and money. Faith is okay with losing power. Say what we want about Peter, he is a man of faith. It took faith for him to leave his boat with the catch of a lifetime to follow Jesus. It took faith for Peter to step out of the boat in the middle of a storm to walk on water to Jesus. And it took faith for Peter as a Jew to go to the home of a Gentile, even though he nursed a ton of questions.

The greatest hitter in baseball history is a man by the name of Pete Rose. The real marvel is not Rose being ranked on the all-time hit list at 4,256 hits but that he got a chance to play in the major leagues at all. Joe Posnanski, in his *New York Times* bestselling book *Baseball 100* says this about Rose:

> Now, look at Pete Rose. He was small. He was awkward. *But he was not cursed with self-awareness*—that's the one thing we know for sure about Rose. The only truth of his childhood, the only thing he completely believed in, was that he was going to be a Major League Baseball player. There was no other option.[5]

What made Rose great is that while all the scouts were fixated on his limitations, he was more aware of the possibilities. Self-awareness, if we are not careful, can be the number one enemy to faith.

Are you "cursed with self-awareness"? Listen, I love personality tests, and I really do think they are valuable. I'm an Enneagram Eight. I'm aware of my love language. I'm a words of affirmation guy. I'm also an introvert, which means tell me how great I am and then leave me alone! Having a handle on your natural wirings is wonderful . . . to a point. Self-awareness can be a curse when it keeps you from walking by faith. Moses was über-self-aware. Unlike most people who aspire to preach, he knew this wasn't his deal. He flat-out told God he couldn't speak and tried to walk away from his calling. Self-awareness can become a real problem because we can be so cognizant of who we are and who we are not that we are blinded to the will of God.

Thank goodness that for all of Peter's wonderful traits, he was not known for self-awareness. Yes, this became a problem at times, but it was also a blessing at others. Had he been fixated on his lack of qualifications for preaching the gospel to Gentiles—the way he was raised, his lack of exposure and experience—he would have turned God down and missed out on God's greater call.

When I think of reliable faith-filled leaders of offensive multiethnic churches, I think of my friend Vance Pitman. I had long heard of Vance and his passion for ethnic unity before I met him face to face. In fact, the first time we talked was on the phone when he invited me to come preach at his church. I mean no harm when I say nothing in Vance's voice said multiethnic. He has a deep Southern drawl bestowed on him by his Muscle Shoals, Alabama, upbringing. He drives a pickup and, worst of all, is a University of Alabama football fan (I am a University of Georgia fan, so I had to throw that in there). You'll forgive me when I tell you that after talking to Vance, I had a "yeah, right" in my spirit. There was just no way he led a truly multiethnic church.

But walking into the service for the first time, I was stunned by the diversity and love the people had. From the worship leader and the songs they sang, to the various kinds of people on the leadership team, to the congregants, it was more than obvious Vance had taken Peter-sized steps to see the vision of ethnic unity birthed in Hope Church, Las Vegas. Vance will also tell you there was hardly anything in his upbringing or training that prepared him to pastor a multiethnic church. All he knew was he wanted to reach all of Vegas with the gospel, and since the city is diverse, his church would have to be too. Had he been cursed with self-awareness over his lack of pedigree or training, he never would have stepped out in faith.

I'll let you in on something—none of us are qualified to fulfill the call of God on our life. Not one of us. There will always be a gap between God's call and our capacity, and the bridge connecting the two is named faith. This is why the most repeated command in the Bible is, "Do not fear," because to step out of the known and familiar and into the unknown is scary. But the same God who was with Peter is with you and I, and just like God honored Peter's faith by using him to lead many Gentiles into the kingdom, God will honor your faith. In fact, here's another thing I've learned from this story, and in my own journey, especially when it comes to ethnic unity: *God responds more to my faith than my questions.* This doesn't mean we don't do our homework. Yes, we should pray and fast and seek clear direction from God. And yes, we should reach out to wise women and men to get their counsel. But I'm telling you, there will come a point where you will still have questions, and you'll just have to take the leap.

RELIABLE LEADERS PUSH THROUGH OPPOSITION

I'm pretty upset with how the story ends. No, I'm not talking about all the Gentiles coming to faith in Jesus. I rejoice over that. I'm talking about the opening lines of Acts 11: "Now the apostles and the brothers who were throughout Judea heard that the Gentiles also had received the word of God. So when Peter went up to Jerusalem, the circumcision party criticized him, saying, 'You went to uncircumcised men and ate with them'" (Acts 11:1-3). This just makes me mad. Here God is supernaturally using Peter as a vessel to bring salvation to the Gentiles, and instead of leaping for joy, the religious elite snarl in criticism. And notice their critique is laced with racism through their mention of "uncircumcised men." The implication here is these Gentiles were beneath them. Did I say this makes me mad?

Every leader worth their salt will face opposition. If you're never getting pushback from people, if you don't have a few people who resist you, I don't think you're leading. It's just the nature of the beast. Moses had his share of grumblers. Nehemiah had Sanballat. Jesus had Judas and the Pharisees. And Peter had the religious leaders.

Nothing exposes people like a fresh vision for ethnic unity. Like turning on a light in a home infested with roaches, going down the path of ethnic unity will illumine hearts overrun by racism. And let me be clear. People were resisting not because Peter was impatient, or hadn't heard from God, or was doing the wrong thing. Remember, Peter is doing exactly what God told him to do. He is right at the epicenter of God's will and still gets opposition. They are resisting because of entrenched ethnic and cultural biases in their hearts. And these are religious people.

For the last four hundred years, racism has been ingrained in the founding and fabric of America. What this means is the gravitational pull of our culture is downward into prejudice, discrimination, and racism. I also believe racism in America is a part of the whole "principalities and powers" language the apostle Paul uses to describe the demonic in Ephesians 6. For any leader to announce a vision of ethnic unity is to invite pushback from both people and the demonic all at once.

Leaders must brace themselves. The opposition will be dizzying. It will come from many of our White brothers and sisters who have a legacy of power and control and have proven they will fight to maintain it. It will come from many minorities who will be impatient, thinking you are not moving fast enough or being forthright in your denunciations. They can also be highly critical and lack grace, not understanding in many cases this is new territory for the leader.

Let me offer a few words of encouragement and hope to you as we round third and head for home. One of the common denominators of great leaders is their attitude. Reliable leaders are filled with hope, not optimism. The latter is based on circumstances. People are optimistic when they buy the lottery ticket or cheer for their sports team. That's not hope. The writer of Hebrews talks about the community of faith having a hope, which is anchored for our souls, and how this anchor is enmeshed in the person of Jesus (Hebrews 6:19). Because Jesus conquered the grave, ascended to heaven, and will return again, we are not fighting for victory, but from victory. Yes, we lament times of racial atrocities, but we do not grieve as those who do not have hope. Reliable leaders can have genuine attitudes of joy even in the face of opposition because they know if God is for them, who can be against them?

Second, assemble a prayer team. Every time I talk to a leader who is looking to cast the new-wine vision of ethnic unity, the first thing I tell them is to pray. This is spiritual warfare, and you will need spiritual artillery. Your vision and strategy without the weapon of prayer is like bringing a knife to a gun fight. Remember, Peter's ministry to the Gentiles in Acts 10 begins at noon on a rooftop when he cries out to God.

Reliable leaders also are never content with outsourcing the vision of ethnic unity; instead, they own the vision of ethnic unity. Of course, you should still put a team together and invest them with power. This is what the leaders do in Acts 6. But a senior leader at a church or organization cannot hire a diversity officer and expect them to do everything while they are not personally invested. People in the organization will listen to the minority leader you've hired, but they will ultimately look to you and how you live as permission for whether they should take what is said seriously.

The final thing I'll offer is reliable leaders are people of conviction. The leaders who most inspire and move people do so not so much with what they say but with how they say things. The Greeks called this *pathos*, which is our idea of passion. To the Greeks, *pathos* was the sense that the leader was speaking from their gut and not just their head. *Pathos* is conviction. *Pathos* can't be faked over the long haul. *Pathos* arises out of a sense of being all in. *Pathos* is being so convinced this person is willing to risk their livelihood, their reputation, and even their life over their conviction.

Martin Luther King Jr., Muhammad Ali, and Nelson Mandela all had *pathos* and risked everything for their convictions. Dr. King literally gave his life fighting racial injustice and what he considered to be the unjust war in Vietnam. The opposition King faced was so vast that just weeks before he died in 1968, the Harris Poll gave him a public disapproval rating of nearly 75 percent.[6] Now, one can hardly go to any city without seeing some street or school named after him. King's contemporary, Muhammad Ali, was also much maligned during the late 1960s because he refused induction into the US army and was very publicly opposed to the war in Vietnam. Had you been a gambler, you would have won a lot of money wagering in the 1960s that Ali would one day be called on to light the Olympic flame, which he did in Atlanta in 1996. Across the pond, Nelson Mandela joined Dr. King and Ali's ranks of resistance when he barely escaped execution for his fight for racial justice and landed in prison on Robben Island, where he was vilified by almost all Afrikaners. Yet, right when Muhammad Ali was lighting the Olympic flame to shouts of praise and adulation, Mandela was well on his way to becoming the most adored person in the world, even though his convictions for racial equality had never changed.

And what about Peter? Well, he's known as one of the pillars of the church, and some sections of the kingdom have even taken their adulation of him to some unnecessary extremes. But this is beside the point. While he may have been deeply discouraged by the opposition he faced from his ethnic kin, the legacy of his ministry was still being written. When the book was closed on his life, he found himself on the right side of history. He was a man of faith who trusted God and played a leading role in seeing Gentiles ushered into the kingdom.

Peter, King, Ali, and Mandela show us an uncanny habit of history: the future is always kind to those who take a stand for what is right, though the present tends to be brutal. No, I am not saying you will reap your reward on this side of heaven. You may very well lose your job and have a low "approval rating" among many. However, we are not laboring for the fleeting praise of people but for the eternal reward of God.

I promise you, a thousand years from now when worshiping at the feet of Jesus, you won't wish you had pacified the status quo in your effort to build or maintain a megachurch. Quite the opposite. You will have wished you had done everything God told you to do despite questions from yourself and others. Do not fear as you leave Paris. The cost is worth every penny.

ETHNIC UNITY DISCUSSION

We've talked a lot about the kind of leader it takes for a church to experience ethnic unity. Would you take a few moments and pray for your pastor? They may have articulated this vision and need boldness. Or they may not have expressed a vision. Pray God burdens their heart for ethnic unity.

Pray God gives your pastor multiethnic friendships.

Pray against discouragement in your pastor's heart, as they will inevitably experience opposition, like Peter, for ethnic unity.

CHAPTER NINE

RELATIONAL ENVIRONMENTS

WHEN NELSON MANDELA WAS ELECTED the first Black president of post-apartheid South Africa, there were deep fears he would use his power to exact revenge. Humanity tends to suffer from long-term memory loss when it comes to Mandela, seeing him only through the prism of a paragon of peace, donning a smile and waving in a show of reconciliation. What we don't remember is the pre–Robben Island Mandela, whose ideology bore a striking resemblance to that of Malcolm X's "by any means necessary" philosophy of justice, a kind of philosophy that led Mandela to resort to violence to draw the nation's attention in his plight for equality.

In this context, it makes sense that on the eve of his inauguration as president, much of the nation and global stage believed Mandela would use his newfound power to get revenge. But these fears were quickly discarded as the new president made his way to his seat at the gala. People could not believe what they were seeing, for Nelson Mandela had invited—no, pleaded with—his White jailor from his years of imprisonment on Robben Island to be seated at his table for this grand occasion. The visual of the Black prisoner seated next to his

White jailor conveyed what was to come: Nelson Mandela was striving far beyond activism. He wanted reconciliation.

ACTIVISM OR RECONCILIATION?

On the journey into ethnic unity, let us not forget there is a difference between activism and reconciliation. Activism focuses on the *what*. Activists fight for things such as police and immigration reform, reparations, and an end to unjust laws like abortion. The great contribution of activists is they have a high sense of fairness and an acute awareness of systemic injustice. It is because of activists I am able to live wherever I want, sit on any seat I'd like on public transportation, and send my children to the school of their choosing. I have lived a very good life because of activists, which is why I say yes and amen to these people. We need godly activists!

But activism becomes a hindrance to ethnic unity when it stops with issues and never gets to people. See, while activists are into the *what*, reconcilers care about the *who* and the *how*. Activists are issue driven, while reconcilers are people driven. Mandela was not just concerned with obliterating old laws and introducing new just ones; he was driven toward bringing oppressed and oppressor, convict and jailor together at the table of reconciliation.

Early on in our marriage, Korie and I befriended a single mother at our church who asked to borrow money from us. It was a substantial amount, especially for a newly married couple establishing their home, but without much discussion we gave her the money with her promising to pay it back. A few months later, she invited us for the first time to dinner at her small apartment. She had obviously forgotten about the money we had loaned her, because while giving us a tour of

the place, she pointed out the new computer she had purchased. I quietly seethed, as not one payment had been made
toward the hard-earned money we had loaned her.

At this moment I had to make a decision—would I allow
the money to be an impediment to the relationship, or would
I risk the relationship by asking for repayment? I have defi-
nitely been on her side of the table before when I was in need
of material help and sensed something was not quite right
about the relationship with the person whose aid I received
until I made restitution. Ideally, activism settles the issue so
the relationship can flourish.

While the Bible speaks to both the activist and the reconciler, the emphasis is always on reconciliation, and not merely
essential activist issues such as restitution. In the Old Testament God talks a lot about restitution, the tangible returning of material to make up for a wrong done. God has a
lot to say about restitution because it sets the table for the
possibility of relationship with the very one who wronged
you. The Israelite family was to pay for another family's
animal that their animal had mauled so there could be the
possibility of relationship. If a person borrowed an object
from another and it was damaged while in their possession,
they were to make restitution so the relationship could
be repaired.

The greatest example of this is the cross. Our sins hindered
a relationship with God. In his justice, he could not overlook
our offenses; payment had to be made. Jesus' death was both
an act of activism and reconciliation in that he satisfied the
wrath of God. Now, not only is the issue resolved but the possibilities for a relationship are open. Activism—calling attention to unjust practices—is beautiful when it leads to

relationship, and therefore unity. However, activism becomes a tool for disunity when it becomes an end unto itself.

One may argue the push for reconciliation did not end at the cross; it only began there. No other book in the New Testament—and quite possibly the whole of Scripture—deals more with the juxtaposition of activism and reconciliation than Paul's concise letter to Philemon.

Philemon is a shocking book, so shocking the great Howard Thurman said in his book *Jesus and the Disinherited* that his grandmother refused to read it because she found it triggering, given her status as a former slave. As we delve into the details, we can more than understand Mother Thurman's allergic reaction to Paul's letter to a slave master entreating him to take back his escaped slave.

Philemon is a wealthy Christ-follower who hosts the church of Colossae in his home. He also owns a slave named Onesimus, who one day decides enough is enough and flees. Some scholars have wondered as to the reason for Onesimus' flight. But do we really need one? There is a universal sense that people should not own people. So Onesimus leaves and makes the one hundred or so mile trek to Rome, where Paul leads him to faith in Christ (Philemon 1:10). I imagine that after a few meetings in which the imprisoned Paul hears his story and disciples him in the faith, Onesimus is shocked to hear Paul's directive that he must go back and make things right with Philemon. To ease the difficulty of such a proposition, Paul writes a letter to Philemon pleading with him to take him back.

You must understand I am a Black man whose ethnicity impacts the way I see the Scriptures. To say I am uneasy with Paul's letter is beyond an understatement.

I want Paul to be far more vociferous in his denunciation of slavery. I want him to scream at Philemon something to the effect of, "What in the world were you thinking? We don't own people, especially as Christians!" And yet, the most we get from Paul is a passing swipe at this "peculiar institution" when he says, "For this perhaps is why he was parted from you for a while, that you might have him back forever, no longer as a bondservant but more than a bondservant, as a beloved brother—especially to me, but how much more to you, both in the flesh and in the Lord" (Philemon 1:15-16). Anyone who tries to make things better by saying, "Now, now, Bryan, slavery in the Bible was not like how it was in the Antebellum South," will be met with a deep breath and an eye roll. People were not created to be owned by other people.

As a Black man, I am frustrated because my bottom line is different from Paul's. I'm after emancipation. Paul is after reconciliation. I want the equivalent of America's Thirteenth Amendment applied to every town and hamlet under first-century Rome's watch. Paul wants Onesimus and Philemon seated at the table of brotherhood. What Paul understands is that there can be emancipation without reconciliation. Doesn't America teach us this? Yes, the Thirteenth Amendment was passed, putting an end to slavery, but were we ever reconciled? What followed (after a brief period known as reconstruction) was Jim Crow. So no, reconciliation did not follow emancipation. Even today, reconciliation eludes us.

Paul knows full well that while we can be emancipated without being reconciled, we can't be truly reconciled without being emancipated. For Philemon to receive Onesimus back "no longer as a bondservant but more than a bondservant, as a beloved brother," would soil and terminate their master-slave dynamic. Reconciliation, the bringing together of former enemies, is the surest way to keep down unjust structures. Of course, I am not pitting emancipation against reconciliation. Let me say it again—we need activists. The Thirteenth Amendment should have happened. Jim Crow needed to be eulogized. We can walk and chew gum all at once. We can fight like activists and eat and laugh like reconciled brothers and sisters. Mandela taught us this.

Need I remind us, the leaders of the civil rights movement were into activism. Their strategy of visible protests—by utilizing the new medium of television in the hopes of afflicting the conscience of America and bringing pressure on our government to bring about change—was all about activism. So, they marched and then boarded airplanes to meet with key governmental leaders to lobby for legislation that would resolve the injustice. But there was more. In the summer of 1961, Dr. King told a primarily White Mississippi audience, "We will wear you down by our capacity to suffer. Do to us what you will and we will still love you. We will meet your physical force with soul force. You may bomb our homes and spit on our children and we will still love you."[1] The key word here is *love*. King and the movement were not just interested in new laws; they wanted relationships. They didn't labor to advocate for changes such as fair housing only to see White flight or gentrification. Instead, they marched and lobbied and advocated so things like fair housing could lead to integrated neighborhoods and dinner tables. Their activism was done with the hope of reconciliation.

I say these things because I am convinced we are at a critical moment in race relations today. One of the many problems we must contend with is an abundance of activists and a scarcity of reconcilers. It appears that too many people want repara-tions, but not enough want relationships with those who have historically wronged us. On the other side of the table, it seems as if so many are opposed to reparations because the relationships with the ones historically wronged aren't a pri-ority. While I do not have the time to launch into a full-scale argument on reparations, I will offer this: a gospel perspective says we should so value people and relationships with them that whatever hinders those relationships should be carefully observed. We must examine all possibilities to remove the im-pediment so we can have fellowship with the other.

WHICH DOOR?

In recent years, much attention has been focused on matters of race, given the video-documented deaths of people of color, often at the hands of police officers. Some people have argued to defund the police. The phrase *critical race theory* is often repeated as well. I am convinced a vast majority of people who use this term do not completely understand what it means outside of the opinion of their preferred media outlet and blogger. Some states have moved to insert more cur-riculum to elevate the race conversation, while other states have gone in the opposite direction. Many local churches that once aspired to move in a multiethnic trajectory have been devastated by reactions on either side of the race conver-sation. Compounding all of this, as noted earlier, is a decline in church attendance by evangelicals. Their discipleship has been diverted from the relational context of the local church to the ideological setting of their favorite news pundit while they sit in isolation at home or in an echo chamber among people who see everything the way they do.

The problem is that many are now embarking on their journey into matters of race through the ideological door and not the relational door. When we only see people through the lens of our opinions and ideologies, we reduce the possibility of ethnic unity and exponentially increase the likelihood for tribalism and division. Plus, people are far more nuanced than our nice little ideological categories. Our Mexican sibling is far more than one's stance on immigration. The wealthy exceed more than what you believe about capitalism. Our Asian sibling is more than one's ideological position on whether systemic forces of injustice are real or if we can simply put our nose to the grindstone, blend in, work hard, and achieve. And the Black person enmeshed in generational poverty should never be reduced to what one believes about welfare, the legacy of slavery, or the need for reparations. Forgive my generalizations, but these examples are meant to divert our attention to a broader point: we are wonderfully complex human beings, so complex we often defy ideological labels. To know me, you can't just read my bio or make assumptions. At some point you must turn off the television and walk with me, and I with you.

The Cuban poet José Martí wrote poignantly along these lines:

> The scorn of our formidable neighbor who does not know us is Our America's greatest danger. And since the day of the visit is near, it is imperative that our neighbor know us, and soon, so that it will not scorn us. Through ignorance it might even come to lay hands on us. Once it does know us, it will remove its hands out of respect. One must have faith in the best of men and distrust the worst.[2]

Martí's words on the preeminence of relationship are so beautiful because he was also a political activist who labored to wrest his native Cuba free from Spain's imperial grip. His words also remind us that he was not merely an activist but a reconciler. He wanted the issue of Spain's dominance removed to allow for the possibility of true relationship.

If the church is going to move from a posture of reaction to one of offense, of proactivity, we must have an army of reconcilers. We must produce people with a singular aim to take up the mantle of the "ministry of reconciliation" by vertically connecting people to God through Christ and horizontally connecting to one another in deeply rich community across the ethnic and ideological divide (2 Corinthians 5:18). The great commandment to love God with the totality of our being and our neighbors as ourselves entails at every turn a deep love for beings, divine and human. Ethnic unity must be entered through the portal of the relational, not the ideological.

The command to love God and people—a command which the whole law rests upon—is also an admission that we are formed most by relationships and that these communities mark us for better or worse. God more than understands this, which is why the three institutions he has ordained for human flourishing—family, government, and church—are all structured relationally in the Scriptures. The first family, Adam and Eve, were naked and unashamed as they journeyed into God's call for oneness in their lives. The government of Israel was set up in a relational structure filled with tribes, clans, and families. And churches were made up mostly of small groups of people who met in homes, shared life with one another, and cared deeply for each other. We've lost this sense of communal attachment and replaced it with what David Brooks calls "hyper-individualism." In his book *The Second Mountain*, Brooks observes,

> Our society suffers from a crisis of connection, a crisis of solidarity. We live in a culture of hyper-individualism. There is always a tension between self and society, between the individual and the group. Over the past sixty years we have swung too far toward the self. The only way out is to rebalance, to build a culture that steers people toward relation, community, and commitment— the things we most deeply yearn for, yet undermine with our hyper-individualistic way of life.[3]

The church, which canvasses the gap from homogeneity to diversity, and from diversity to ethnic unity, will create relational environments that go to war with "hyper-individualism." The Covid-19 pandemic exposed local churches that were previously content driven in their paradigm for ministry—you know, the kinds of churches that were more weekend services than they were churches. Once the pandemic struck and people holed up at home, those pastors found competition with some of the best communicators in the world, all made available via the internet. I fear we have not come out of the buffet line of sermons our smart televisions and devices afford us. Call me an incurable optimist, but I see this as much of an opportunity as it is an obstacle. The church of the future is now being forced to become relational if it has any hopes of thriving. Our need for belonging is a deeply felt one, and if the multiethnic church is going to galvanize and thrive, it must be relational.

COMMON GROUND

Jesus' incarnation did not occur within a hyper-individu-alized society; however, he did face a racial barrier that challenged the advancement of his kingdom program. Jews and Samaritans did not get along, often for ethnic reasons. Samaritans were a mixture of Jew and Greek, and the average Jew so despised the Samaritans' perceived ethnic impurity they looked down their nose and referred to them as dogs. Much has been said about how no self-respecting Jew in Jesus' day would have even passed through Samaria. Theirs was a culture of avoidance, and it is within this cultural moment that Jesus had to pass through Samaria (John 4:4). However, Jesus not only passed through but also stopped to have a conversation with a Samaritan woman of ill repute at a well. This conversation would prove transformative for her life and the life of her town, as the kingdom of heaven would break out in the most unlikely of places. The culmination of these events would lead to her and many others' reconciliation to Christ, along with Jesus modeling horizontal reconciliation across the racial chasm. The source for this vertical and horizontal outburst of reconciliation was time spent at a relational environment known as a well. Jesus' method of transformation was relational and not ideological.

We can never overestimate the power of relationships in changing people. Any local church that harbors aspirations of ethnic unity must figure out how to provide "wells" within the fabric of their ecclesia so we can sit and exchange with one another across the many barriers that have estranged us. Studying the life of Jesus, we know the kingdom did not only come from stages and sermons but also around tables and wells. Read the Gospels and we will see that while the masses were informed from afar, people were transformed up close at dinner parties, late night conversations, boat rides across the sea, weddings, and wells.

The race problem exists because the relationship distance persists. We need to pull each other close. Yes, sitting together on a pew in a multiethnic service is nice, but sitting around a table with a plate is even better. The sermon might inform our minds, but the dinner table will warm our hearts. I am not placing one over the other; I am saying we need both. We need relationships with one another.

FULLY HUMAN

At this well, a conversation ensues between two drastically different people. One is male, the other female. One is the Messiah, the other is a woman who is the subject of gossip, much of it well earned. And of course, one is Jewish and the other Samaritan. The woman has come to draw water at the sixth hour of the day, and since the first hour of the day according to Jewish custom was six in the morning, it is now noon. Everyone knows people come to draw water in the morning because it is much cooler out, but she is here in the heat because she wants to avoid the scorn that has followed her for many years. She is pensive as she comes to the well. And it's here where Jesus asks her for water.

His request is shocking for many reasons, not least of which because a Jewish man has chosen to speak to her. Not quite sure what to say, she lets the words pour out of her. How is it that he, a Jew, would ask her for water? Doesn't Jesus know the rules? Jewish men don't speak to Samaritans. But wait a minute, how does she know Jesus is a Jew? Jesus didn't announce himself as one. We can only conclude he must have been dressed like a Jew. He must have talked like a Jew. In his humanity, Jesus was completely comfortable in his Jewishness.

So here is Jesus, unashamed of being a Jew and completely comfortable in his own skin. At the same time, Jesus honors the humanity of this Samaritan woman by breaking cultural norms to engage her. So, they sit together—one completely Jew, the other completely Samaritan. Both bring the totality of who they are to the well.

If we are going to journey beyond diversity and into ethnic unity, we need wells where each person can bring the fullness of their humanity. We have no hope for this journey if people must leave their Latino/a or Chinese embodied selves at the door (to name some examples). If the rules for the well entail being colorblind, we will not sit down together for long.

In some sense, we get the need to honor one another's humanity, don't we? The example Christ sets for us in John 4 as an embodied Jewish ethnic minority cements the notion that people do not have to divest themselves of their ethnicity to follow Christ. But this does not only apply to people of color; it also applies to our White siblings. We must be very careful with language like "repent of your Whiteness." Even if this refers to the sinful acts of supremacy that are often attached to Whiteness, I would still appeal for more specific language. If we can affirm one's color and ethnicity are a part of what it means to be created in the image of God, then does that not also apply to our White siblings? If so, we likewise need to invite them to sit at the well with us in their embodied selves. And yes, there are aspects of every ethnicity that need to be brought under the conformity of Christ, namely ethnic idolatry, so you will permit me a little grace as time does not allow me to explore this as deeply as I'd like.

We need our White brothers and sisters at the well with us, or we have no hope of ethnic unity with them. To mix my metaphors, we do not need our White *familia* to be seated at the head of the table. In fact, the table is a circular one, where there is no superior (outside of Christ) or inferior. As my friend Robert Guerrero says, this is an "us space."

HEAR THEIR STORY

Beware, though, sitting in the "us space" of wells and dinner tables will entail awkward moments. We see this in Jesus' conversation with the Samaritan woman when he mentions that she has been with five different men and the one she is with now is not her husband. This is painful, and let's be honest, most of us would have just left this out altogether. What's clear, and ultimately transformative, is Jesus is saying she doesn't need to hide or pretend everything is fine when it is not. He knows her story.

Relational environments that push the conversation from diversity into ethnic unity must be spaces where we take the time to hear one another's stories. Just like the afternoon Korie drove our boys and me around for hours sharing stories and showing us places from her childhood, so we also need to carve out the time to learn about each other's stories. Not because it's something nice to do or because it's politically correct, but because we are family and love one another. When you love someone, you want to learn about them.

Of course, there are multiple levels to this. On a broad level, we learn about each other's narratives when we participate in Lunar New Year, Cinco de Mayo, or Black History Month. These moments are important because to engage them is to convey that we care. We also grow and become better human beings in the process.

HEAR THE STORY

Not long into their conversation, we come to understand this well has a name: Jacob's Well. Our Samaritan friend is right to point out the place of affection Jacob holds in the hearts of her ethnic kin. And of course, Jacob, being one of the Jewish patriarchs, holds a similar place of honor among the Jews. Thus, the place they have convened is common ground.

Notice that what brought them to the well was the much larger narrative of their father, Jacob. What kept them at the well and changed their lives was an even grander narrative known as the gospel. Ethnicity played a much-needed supporting role, but it was by no means the star.

Morgan Snyder observes, "We cannot live beyond the identity we have embraced."[4] Ethnicity is way too low of an identity in our pursuit of human flourishing. It is a necessary part of who we are, but it can never fully satisfy the deepest longings of our hearts. The "living water" Jesus offers this woman in his promise to satisfy her thirst does not provide a fuller understanding of her makeup as a Samaritan but focuses on the infrastructure of her heart. Notice, Jesus honors her humanity on the way to her soul, because our soul informs our ethnicity and not the other way around. We see this in the life of Jesus. He didn't come to merely learn about what life was like as a Samaritan. The gospel navigated his journey.

My wife and I are in an interracial relationship. Early on in our marriage, we were invited to the home of an interracial couple from our church. Midway through our meal, it dawned on me that everyone around the table was likewise in a multiethnic relationship. We talked about the challenges we experienced and enjoyed an all-around rich time together. Afterward, someone had the idea of making this a regular gathering where we would continue to encourage one another as interracial couples. We got together a few more times, and the dialogue revolved solely around how "hard" it was for all of us. There was no gospel. No Bible study. No metanarrative to hook into. After a few more meetings, Korie and I tapped out. We had already decided to not live as if people were always against us. For example, if we were out to eat and someone was staring at us, I would assume I had surely spilled ketchup on my shirt. While we have decided to not be naive, we have also made the choice to not assume the worst in people. What a miserable way to live and a guarantor of perpetual anger and angst. No thank you.

Please don't misunderstand me. What I have shared is specific to where I was in my walk with Christ and our needs as a couple. There are many who would glean great value from groups like the one we test drove. But it is also important to remember we all have felt needs and deeper needs. Just as Jesus took the felt need of water and belonging this woman ached for and stitched it to the deeper need of the gospel, so we also need to be careful to connect our ethnicity to the metanarrative of the living water of Jesus Christ. We need something beyond us to inform and empower our ethnicity and multiethnic marriage and family. We need the living water of the Holy Spirit and the transformative message of the gospel if there is to be any hope of human flourishing.

I've also learned over the years it is just not good for my soul if I constantly read books on race. Yes, I need to be informed to do my job well. But I have found I reach a certain point where I run a bit of a fever with my White brothers and sisters after imbibing a certain number of these books consecutively. When I pay too much attention to the flesh, I realize my mind is no longer being transformed by the Scriptures but by the pen of sociologists. So, I take a break. We do need to talk about race, but we need to do so as a part of the metanarrative of God's redemptive grace and gospel worked out toward every nation, tribe, and tongue.

When we stitch race and ethnicity to the gospel, we open ourselves up to talk about forgiveness. We make it virtually impossible to go the way of cancel culture and instead do the work of reconciliation. When we fly at the higher altitude of the good news of Jesus Christ, we are ready to extend grace and display the insignia of love. And I've also discovered a beautiful side effect of the gospel—it gives me increased energy and stamina to walk with people who do not get it when it comes to matters of race.

READY/RELUCTANT/RESISTANT

There is a danger to relational environments seeking to talk about the gospel and race because they become pep rallies where everyone is on the same exact page. We don't move the needle when we only gather with people who see it the way we do. We need people who are at very different points in the race conversation, because that is where empathy develops, relationships are strengthened, and growth happens.

I once was talking to my mother about these matters when she pointed out there are three different types of people when it comes to the gospel and race: the ready, the reluctant, and the resistant. In my years of working with churches to grow in ethnic unity, I found my mother's observation to be accurate. These people are a part of most churches, and as we think about establishing our network of wells within the local body of Christ, we should think through having representation, especially among the ready and the reluctant, in each group.

I do hesitate about having the resistant in your relational environment because they will either turn down the invitation to sit at the well or cause great turmoil in the group. While everyone needs to be approached pastorally, once a person digs in and proves themself to be immovable along these delicate lines, you may need to encourage them to pursue other endeavors. The great writer Maya Angelou once pointed out that when a person shows you who they are, you should believe them. And so when someone shows themselves resistant to matters of race and the gospel, believe them.

Social media and the overwhelming number of viewing options on TV and the internet have allowed me to craft a world where I surround myself only with people who see things the way I do. If I don't like your comment, I can block you. I can unfollow you if you post something I disagree with. I can choose to only watch media outlets that affirm my presuppositions. This means we are being formed more ideologically than relationally with those who see things differently. I fear we will use this same approach with small groups by gathering people who only hold our same point of view. This is not the way of Jesus, who built quite the eclectic group of followers. Simon the Zealot did life with Levi the tax collector. It doesn't get more different.

As you think about your wells, invite people who are ethnically and ideologically different. Set a term limit, such as agreeing to meet for a year. Keep the bar of commitment high

and set ground rules for how everyone will communicate
with one another given the flammable nature of the topic of
race. Pray together. Make it clear you are not trying to change
anyone's views on politics, money, or ideology. Show them
how ethnic unity is central to God's heart and the origins of
the local church. Create space for people to share their narrative. Resist the urge to change anyone. That is not our call.
We cannot even change ourselves. Be respectful of the various
ethnic and cultural philosophies of community. Some groups
are more time- and agenda-focused, while others are more
people-focused. Emphasize the importance of the Spirit-
filled life. Seize moments of national crises around race as
opportunities for lament. Share leadership. Read the Bible
together. Did I say pray together?

If you do these things, you will discover over time that the
ready will grow in empathy toward the reluctant and resistant,
and vice versa. You will see a softening and an openheart-
edness replace dogmatic opinions and harsh language. I say
this with confidence because I have seen it myself.

In the early days of our church in Memphis, a young,
wealthy White family joined. By their own admission, they
had not grown up with any kind of ethnic or socioeconomic
diversity. Quite the opposite. But sure enough, God began
working on their hearts, and the vision of diversity—along
with our church's culture of people loving one another across
the ethnic divide—captivated their hearts. Over time, their
extended family began to trickle in and lock arms with us.

I watched in awe as the members of this affluent White
family formed deep, authentic friendships with minorities.
Their new friends both loved them and challenged their presuppositions and biases. Soon, they began to listen and take

radical steps of reconciliation. Some used their money to economically empower others. Another one decided to enroll in an HBCU to learn from professors of color. And still another chose to adopt cross-ethnically. All of this happened because of the impact of a gospel-saturated, multiethnic community.

CONCLUSION

In the aftermath of George Floyd, athletic teams seized the cultural moment and led the way in lament, empathy, and pleas for justice. Many of these teams are diverse, and compared to the average church in America, small. Some of these teams are the size of your small groups. They know each other. They've sat in locker rooms with one another. They've seen each other's best days and worst days. They've helped each other off the court when someone is injured and congratulated each other when someone makes the game-winning shot. If they've experienced any measure of success, it's because theirs is a deeply relational culture.

The larger narrative of competition brought them together. Along the way, they spent uncountable hours in practice and games, all working toward the same objective. Within this larger movement was the subplot of race. There's something to be said about seeing one of your teammates who you go to war with on the field of competition hurting deeply over some racial tragedy. And so they stood side by side on basketball courts and baseball diamonds as one unified team, lamenting, protesting, and pleading. They were one. Their togetherness was stimulated by their mutual commitment to one another to play for something larger than what any one individual could achieve on the team: a championship.

I'm not here to say we need to mimic their every move and go out and buy "Black Lives Matter" T-shirts. I am saying we need to copy their commitment to one another. As the church, the people of God, we are playing for something far greater than an earthly trophy or ring. We are playing with eternity in mind. This is our moment. And what we need are churches filled with wells—gathering spots where we know and are known. Part of this adventure into one another's stories is that we learn what life is like in another person's skin. There, empathy happens, unity is stimulated, and we can truly begin to play offense and storm the gates of hell.

ETHNIC UNITY DISCUSSION

Thinking of your small group as a well where you can have multiethnic conversations, have you been able to bring the fullness of yourself ethnically to the well? If you are White, do you find yourself consistently holding back what you think because of your white skin? If you are a minority, do you find yourself holding back because you don't want to rock the boat? Talk about these things in your group.

While ethnic unity is an essential discussion, how well does your group connect the subplot of race to the metanarrative of the gospel?

EPILOGUE

FOR ALMOST ALL OF my professional life, I have given myself to seeing the multiethnic church become the new normal in our society. Up until a few years ago, my primary service to the cause was proactively resourcing aspiring leaders in how to lead these sorts of churches. However, with the election of Donald Trump, followed by the many video-documented incidents of minority deaths at the hands of police officers, I have found myself playing more of an emergency room doctor helping fractured multiethnic churches survive. There's only so much trauma one can witness without being personally demoralized. I've often had moments where I've wondered if my labor is in vain.

At the height, or rather the depth, of all this pain and division, I was called on to lecture at a seminary in the South on the multiethnic church. It was one of those moments where I had to manufacture hope, forcing myself to come across like I believed what I was really saying, I was that down. Later that evening, I was invited to hang out with some of the other instructors and administrators on the grounds of this Southern school. The conversation inevitably turned to the subject of racial division, with some wondering if we would indeed survive this moment.

Finally, the president of the seminary stood up and pointed to a headstone just a few feet away from us. With conviction, he asked us if we knew who was buried there. Somewhat unsettled that there was a dead body beneath the cobblestone of the courtyard where we had convened, I shrugged and said we had no idea.

He explained that this was the corpse of the original owner of the land the seminary had purchased; it was also the original owner of the building where I had just taught my students. Oh, and this person had once been an owner of slaves. Letting out his boisterous laugh, my friend and seminary president helped us to connect the dots: the seminary that had begun in order to equip urban leaders, many of whom aspire to be a part of the multiethnic church, was doing this kingdom work on once slave-holding land. The kingdom of darkness had been defeated, and we were reclaiming territory for the glory of God. We were on the offensive.

As our night came to an end, I let my mind go back further than the events of recent years. I thought of my great-great-grandfather, Peter, who was a slave in North Carolina. He could never imagine any of his descendants leading a multiethnic church, much less teaching ethnic unity on the grounds once occupied by slaves. He would certainly scold me for feeling down on myself as if no progress has been made. We have made progress.

God's church—his multiethnic church—is advancing. We are on the move. God will continue to raise up workers to continue his offensive program here on earth until he returns. We are not working for victory, but from victory.

ACKNOWLEDGMENTS

I AM GRATEFUL TO the people of Summit Church, who lovingly extended the invitation to our family to come and help lead our efforts into ethnic unity. I have found them to be eager and very open. I have written this book with this family in mind, and my hope is we will return to the principles embedded in these pages over the years to come.

To my new friends at IVP, it has been a joy to partner with you in this project. InterVarsity has a long and well-earned track record of ethnic unity and providing authors of color with a platform to articulate our ideas, all with the aim of pushing the body of Christ and broader culture further. Al Hsu in particular has been so helpful in providing content feedback for this work, and the book is better for it.

When I first mentioned the idea for this project to my agent, Andrew Wolgemuth, he provided great encouragement and as always pushed me to crystallize my ideas. Andrew isn't just a godly man and an exceptional agent; he has given of himself personally to the offensive church and the fight for ethnic unity. We have worked together for well over a decade, and I hope we have many more years to come.

I am what is affectionately known as middle-aged, which means the ideas I had regarding ethnic unity (along with a host of others) were in need of refreshening. I have felt this for some time and therefore have surrounded myself with much younger siblings in Christ, who have taken up the mantle of reconciliation. Women and men like Ade and Janetta Oni, Charles Holmes, Oscar Wilburn, Yana Conner, and others have played a pivotal role in orienting me to the mind of millennials and Gen Z in regard to these matters. They have been so helpful, and I am indebted.

Most important are my wife, Korie, and our children, Quentin, Myles, and Jaden. Korie has never been one for the stage and bright lights; she likes it more behind the scenes, and it's there where she has been our family's greatest encouragement in matters of diversity and ethnic unity. All three of our sons are heading into the young adult phase of life. One of them asked me recently if I knew of any good multiethnic churches in his area. Another expressed discomfort that his current church where he enjoys the preaching and some of the programs does not seem to be pushing hard enough in this area. They have grown up with a new normal, and having acquired a taste for the beloved community, it's hard for them to venture anywhere else.

NOTES

INTRODUCTION: WHAT'S GOING ON?

[1] James Davison Hunter, Carl Desportes Bowman, and Kyle Puetz, *Democracy in Dark Times*, IASC Survey of American Political Culture (Charlottesville, VA: Finstock & Tew, 2020), 57.

2. SEEING THROUGH THE FOG

[1] Randy Alcorn, "Florence Chadwick and the Fog," Eternal Perspective Ministries, January 21, 2010, www.epm.org/resources/2010/Jan/21/florence -chadwick-and-fog.

[2] Niara Savage, "'It Was a Slap in the Face': Black Couple's Home Valuation Increased by 50 Percent After White Friend Posed as Homeowner During the Inspection," *Atlanta Black Star,* February 16, 2021, https://atlantablackstar .com/2021/02/16/it-was-a-slap-in-the-face-black-couples-home-valuation -increased-by-50-percent-after-white-friend-posed-as-homeowner-during -the-inspection.

[3] Jay Caspian Kang, *The Loneliest Americans* (New York: Crown, 2021), 203-4.

[4] Eugene H. Peterson, *Working the Angles: The Shape of Pastoral Integrity* (Grand Rapids, MI: Eerdmans, 1990), 67.

[5] Sarah Shin, *Beyond Colorblind: Redeeming Our Ethnic Journey* (Downers Grove, IL: InterVarsity Press, 2017), 54-55.

[6] Miroslav Volf, *The End of Memory* (Grand Rapids, MI: Eerdmans, 2006), 146.

[7] Volf, *End of Memory*, 19.

[8] Jon Meacham, *His Truth Is Marching On: John Lewis and the Power of Hope* (New York: Random House, 2021), 66.

[9] Meacham, *His Truth Is Marching On,* 91.

3. COMMUNAL IDENTITY AND ETHNIC UNITY

[1] John Dickson, *Bullies and Saints: An Honest Look at the Good and Evil of Christian History* (Grand Rapids, MI: Zondervan, 2021), 93.

[2] Dickson, *Bullies and Saints*, 98.

[3] Dickson, *Bullies and Saints*, 93.

[4] Robert P. Jones, *The End of White Christian America* (New York: Simon and Schuster, 2016), 136, emphasis added.

[5] Wikipedia, s.v. "The dress," last edited November 21, 2022, https://en.wikipedia.org/wiki/The_dress.

[6] Korie L. Edwards, *The Elusive Dream: The Power of Race in Interracial Churches* (New York: Oxford University Press, 2008), 37.

[7] Ken Burns, *Jazz*, "The Adventure," PBS, 2004, www.pbs.org/kenburns/jazz/.

[8] Miroslav Volf, *The End of Memory: Remembering Rightly in a Violent World* (Grand Rapids, MI: Eerdmans, 2006), 30-31.

4. THE PRACTICES OF ETHNIC UNITY

[1] Andrew Murray, *Humility: The Beauty of Holiness* (Fort Washington, PA: Christian Literature Crusade, 2012), 7.

[2] Spiros Zodhiates, *The Complete Word Study Dictionary: New Testament* (Chattanooga, TN: AMG, 1993), Logos Research ed., s.v. "*prautes*."

5. BEWARE OF A NEW VISION WITH AN OLD CULTURE

[1] Richard Wright, *Black Boy (American Hunger): A Record of Childhood and Youth* (New York: Harper Perennial, ill. ed., 2020), 264.

[2] Wright, *Black Boy*, 196.

[3] David Brooks, "The Dissenters Trying to Save Evangelicalism from Itself," *New York Times*, February 4, 2022, www.nytimes.com/2022/02/04/opinion/evangelicalism-division-renewal.html.

[4] See Peter Scazzero, *Emotionally Healthy Spirituality*, updated ed. (Grand Rapids, MI: Zondervan, 2017).

[5] M. Robert Mulholland Jr., *Invitation to a Journey*, rev. and exp. ed. (Downers Grove, IL: InterVarsity Press, 2016), 16, emphasis added.

[6] Cornel West (@CornelWest), "Justice is what love looks like in public," Twitter, October 17, 2018, 10:41 a.m., https://twitter.com/cornelwest/status/1052585306916974592?lang=en.

[7] Gordon MacDonald, *A Resilient Life: You Can Move Ahead No Matter What* (Nashville: Thomas Nelson, 2006), 194.

[8] C. S. Lewis, *The Four Loves* (New York: HarperOne, 2017), Kindle, 82.

[9] C. S. Lewis, *Mere Christianity* (New York: HarperOne, 2001), 216.

6. PROCLAIMING A ROBUST GOSPEL

[1] Cecil M. Robeck, *The Azusa Street Mission and Revival: The Birth of the Global Pentecostal Movement* (Nashville: Thomas Nelson, 2017), 319.

[2] Carl F. H. Henry, *The Uneasy Conscience of Modern Fundamentalism* (Grand Rapids, MI: Eerdmans, 2003), loc. 82 of 726, Kindle.

[3]Henry, *The Uneasy Conscience*, loc. 136 of 726, Kindle.

[4]Henry, *The Uneasy Conscience*, loc. 104 of 726, Kindle.

[5]Henry, *The Uneasy Conscience*, loc. 231 of 726, Kindle.

[6]"Prego: It's in There," Commercial Heaven (website), May 4, 2007, https://commercialheaven.com/2007/05/04/prego-its-in-there.

7. PRACTICING A ROBUST GOSPEL

[1]Dietrich Bonhoeffer, *Life Together* (New York: HarperOne, 1978), 27.

[2]From Scot McKnight's *A Fellowship of Differents*, repr. ed. (Grand Rapids, MI: Zondervan, 2016).

[3]Cecil M. Robeck, *The Azusa Street Mission and Revival: The Birth of the Global Pentecostal Movement* (Nashville: Thomas Nelson, 2017), 216-19.

[4]Matt Chandler, "Racial Harmony," sermon, The Village Church, January 22, 2019, YouTube video, 42:11, www.youtube.com/watch?v=BODXTG_j3yc.

[5]Bryan Loritts, *Kainos: Seeking the Multiethnic Church with Dr. Bryan Loritts* (podcast), The Summit Church, Durham, NC, accessed November 29, 2022, https://podcasts.apple.com/us/podcast/kainos-seeking-the-multiethnic-church-with-dr/id1595620088.

8. RELIABLE LEADERSHIP

[1]Eddie S. Glaude Jr., *Begin Again: James Baldwin's America and Its Urgent Lessons for Our Own* (New York: Crown, 2020), 29-30

[2]Glaude Jr., *Begin Again*, 31.

[3]Allister Sparks, *Tomorrow Is Another Country: The Inside Story of South Africa's Road to Change* (Chicago: University of Chicago Press, 1996), 106.

[4]Sparks, *Tomorrow Is Another Country*, 100.

[5]Joe Posnanski, *The Baseball 100* (New York: Avid Reader Press, 2021), 266, emphasis added.

[6]James C. Cobb, "Even Though He Is Revered Today, MLK Was Widely Disliked by the American Public When He Was Killed," *Smithsonian Magazine*, April 4, 2018, www.smithsonianmag.com/history/why-martin-luther-king-had-75-percent-disapproval-rating-year-he-died-180968664.

9. RELATIONAL ENVIRONMENTS

[1]Jon Meacham, *His Truth is Marching On: John Lewis and the Power of Hope* (New York: Random House, 2020), 115.

[2]Quoted in Juan Gonzalez, *Harvest of Empire: A History of Latinos in America*, rev. ed. (New York: Penguin, 2011), vii.

[3]David Brooks, *The Second Mountain: The Quest for a Moral Life* (New York: Random House, 2020), xvii.

[4]Morgan Snyder, *Becoming a King* (Nashville: Thomas Nelson, 2021), 55.

ABOUT THE AUTHOR

BRYAN C. LORITTS (DMin, Liberty University) is the teaching pastor at The Summit Church, along with serving as the vice president for regions for the Send Network, the church planting arm of the SBC, where he is responsible for training church planters in multiethnic church planting. He cofounded Fellowship Memphis in 2003 and serves as president of The Kainos Movement, an organization committed to seeing the multiethnic church become the new normal.

His ministry takes him across the globe annually, as he speaks at conferences, churches, and retreats. Bryan has been a featured speaker for Catalyst and the Global Leadership Summit. He was teaching pastor of The Summit Church, serves on the boards of Biola University, and is a regular visiting professor at Grimke Seminary. His books include *Insider Outsider*, *A Cross-Shaped Gospel*, *The Dad Difference*, and *Right Color, Wrong Culture*.

He is the husband of Korie and the father of Quentin, Myles, and Jaden.

https://bryanloritts.com/

🐦 DrLoritts

📷 @loritts

📘 DrBryanLoritts

Podcast: *Kainos: Seeking the Multiethnic Church*

https://podcasts.apple.com/us/podcast/kainos-seeking-the-multiethnic-church-with-dr/id1595620088